# Let's Go!

## FEARLESS EVANGELISM

How to share the Gospel in
everyday life.

# HELEN DEVENISH

Ark House Press
PO Box 1722, Port Orchard, WA 98366 USA
PO Box 1321, Mona Vale NSW 1660 Australia
PO Box 318 334, West Harbour, Auckland 0661 New Zealand
arkhousepress.com

Cataloguing in Publication Data:
Title: Let's Go!
ISBN: 978-0-6480500-0-1 (pbk.)
Subjects: Evangelism, Mission, Christian Living
Other Authors/Contributors: Devenish, Helen

Cover Design by Thomas Devenish
Sketches on cover by Helen Devenish
Layout by initiateagency.com

lovehobart@gmail.com
www.lovehobart.com

To my husband David who has encouraged me every step of the way
to be all that the Lord has purposed for me to be,
along with our children. Go team Devenish!

# Contents

# Foreword

How Do Followers of Jesus Reach Their Greatest Potential? It was early 1981, and I was just halfway through my first year at Messiah College. My ambition had been to stay on the farm in Maryland, but God had other plans for me. On one of my visits back home to the farm I sought the Lord about my future direction, and He gave me a strong impression to pursue Christian Education as my major. It was at that point that I felt a solid calling into how the Lord would use me for the rest of my life. After those years of university, I felt that learning was the key to reaching my potential.

Along the way in my life journey, I occasionally stumbled upon evangelists. I suppose that, growing up in modern-day Christianity, we may think evangelists are the odd ones in the body of Christ; the exception to the rule. "I could never do what they do" was my rationale for years. I rested firmly on my resolve to keep learning and to keep my faith to myself.

It wasn't until several years later that I began to learn that evangelism is not for the select few. Even a brief look at Acts quickly reminds us that sharing our faith is the norm, not the exception, in every disciple's life. But the fact remains that too many believers look for alternatives to sharing their faith. My wife has said many times in jest, "I'll do anything, anything at all, to lose weight except eat healthy and exercise." Sadly, that seems to typify the way many believers think about the Great Commission. We seem to be so good at making excuses while looking for an easier alternative.

We have before us in the pages that follow, a stirring reminder that evangelism is something for all of us who are Christ's.

Helen provides for us an impassioned plea to step out in faith and share the wonderful news of Jesus. Perhaps one expects at this point some commentary and affirmation on what she has written here. Her stories, methods, and motivation in this book are priceless. But permit me to discuss something even more precious: the person herself.

It has been a privilege to meet Helen and to experience someone uniquely shaped by God. Rarely do I meet someone with such a drive to proclaim the Gospel message face-to-face, with people who are far from God. She exudes energy that manifests her love for the Lord Jesus and His mission.

I love Helen's obedience to God and her willingness to model bold witness. While indeed she is gifted in evangelism, what she does is not so much about gifting as it is responding to the Father's heart for a lost and broken world. Evangelism for her is not a compartmentalised activity, but an expression of her heart for God wherever she goes; it is for her not merely a vocation, but an expression of who she is on the inside.

Helen is a woman of great faith. Vision is the ability to see what God sees, and faith is truly believing it can happen— childlike trust that God actually has the ability to do what He says He will do—and offering wholehearted service in partnering with Him. Such faith is an unquenchable fire that continually says, "God can do it!"

She is also a person with great persistence.Over the years, we watched her respond to spiritual warfare—and she has had to face a lot of it, as you will see in these pages. Most people would have given up after the first few waves of resistance. But Helen never backed down from her calling and commitment to God, proving to be an amazing example of courage in the face of impossible situations.

Among the most painful experiences of my life was to leave Tasmania after nearly 18 years—a third of my life at that point in time. God's call was crystal clear to us, and we knew it was time to leave. But knowing that people like Helen and her family were in Australia gave us peace in moving to London.

And now, we return to the question, "How do followers of Jesus reach their greatest potential?" We grow into Christlikeness not by merely learning the Word and growing in knowledge, but by passing it on to others. Sharing the Gospel and training disciples to go and make other disciples is the rocket fuel of our faith, and it is this releasing of the Kingdom message into the hands of others that continues to take me to places I had never imagined. Sadly, the vast majority of believers never get past that first hurdle of learning to share their simple faith story with others.

My recommendation is that you start reading this book, then mark the page and go and find someone you know who is far from God and share something of the wonderful works of God in your own life. You'll begin to understand in a new way not just the amazing value of His Word, but the indescribable joy that is found only when you start giving it away.

**Ben Armacost** April 2017,
London, UK Founder, AIM Trainers
(aimtrainers.org) Author of *Bridge to the Beautiful City*

"And Jesus came and spoke to them, saying, "All authority has been given to Me in Heaven and on earth. Go therefore and make disciples of all the nations, baptizing them in the name of the Father and of the Son and of the Holy Spirit, teaching them to observe all things that I have commanded you: and lo, I am with you always, even to the end of the age. Amen"

*Matthew 28:18-20*

"While prophetic interpretations are fascinating, don't let them become a distraction from your commission- to preach the Gospel to every creature (Mark 16:15). We have too many who run from conference to conference, filling their mind with theories to a point where they have neither time, nor concern, for those who could be snatched any moment into eternal damnation."

*Ray Comfort*

# Introduction

So many Christians want to prophesy, and indeed we are encouraged to desire to prophesy above all else *(1 Corinthians 14:1)*, but what about a desire to evangelise? Jesus commanded Christians to "GO into all the world and preach the Gospel", yet so few are actually doing it. There doesn't seem to be a long line up of people desiring to go and preach the Gospel to the lost. Evangelism seminars are never as well attended as prophetic seminars. But the final command of Jesus was to "GO and preach the Gospel". If you're a Christian that means YOU!

In September 2010 my daughter Joanne had a prophecy for me. She saw a net bursting with fish and had the word that I was to cast my net on the other side of the boat. I had no idea how I was to do that, so I started praying about it. I asked the Lord to show me what He meant for me to do. Obviously, it was going to be different to anything I was doing at the time. I continued to ask the Lord, "how am I to cast my net on the other side?" This is where my journey into evangelism began. God was about to send me out to the people, the lost souls of Hobart. The first step was through running an outreach café and then, a couple of years' later, street ministry became the focus.

Are you ready and willing to cast your net on the other side? God may not send you out onto the streets of your city, but He may send you to an old people's home, a shopping mall, a bus, a park, a beach, a gym or a ride in a taxi. Everyday there are people you meet who don't know Jesus. Are you willing to say to the Lord, 'I'll go anywhere for you?' Are you willing to open your mouth and tell the people in your life about

Jesus? If not, then you need to get a passion for the lost, for this is the heart of the Father.

*"For God did not send His Son into the world to condemn the world, but that the world through Him might be saved." John 3:17*

Remember the lost are heading towards Hell. The heart of the Father is that none should perish. Is that your heart too? If not, why not? If you know the Father through His Son, Jesus, then your desires should reflect our God. You need to get to know Jesus more and find out how much He loves the lost, but also know how much He can be trusted when you step out of your comfort zone to preach the Gospel to this lost generation.

Don't let anything hold you back from being obedient to the Great Commission of Jesus to 'GO'!

And guess what? When you're obeying Jesus' commandment to GO, it's amazing what an adventure it becomes! It's such an awesome privilege and blessing to share the Good News of the Gospel of Jesus especially in these days, when so many of the younger generation have NEVER heard the Gospel before. Also, every time you share the Gospel you encourage yourself as you're reminded by your very words of the power of the cross and the resurrection of Jesus.

It's so much easier to share the best Good News there is, than sharing bad news. Our world is full of bad news, so let's GO and share the Good News everywhere we go.

Play (who can relate to this?)

*Adam-* Now, who'd like to come and do some street ministry with me? Beck?

*Beck-* Oh, I don't know?

*Adam-* Yes, come on, you can do it. I'll train you.

*Beck-* Oh, ok, I guess so.

*Adam-* Great! So we're going to go and approach people and ask them if we can share the Gospel. To start with I'll do the talking and you can just watch how I do it. You can learn a lot that way.

*Beck-* Ok, that doesn't sound too hard I guess.

*Adam-* Ok, let's go!

*Beck-* I'm scared!!

*Adam-* What are you scared of?

*Beck-* Well, what will people think? What if they get angry with us? What if they ask us something we can't answer?

*Adam-* And what if we don't do it, what will God think? And people generally don't get angry if you're polite and respectful to them. And if you don't know the answer to a question say you don't know. You don't have to know everything. You see Beck, the thing is, Jesus commanded us to go into all the world and preach the Gospel, and I'm here to help train you, so all you have to do is come with me. I won't leave you by yourself, you just need to see how I do it and then one day soon, when you're confident enough, you'll be able to do it yourself. But for now it's just baby steps. And remember, God is with us. He will help us. As we walk with Him, and spend time with Him, you and I will both become bolder.

*Beck-* Are you sure?

*Adam-* Yes. Read *Acts 4*. How many times is boldness mentioned there? And what does *verse 31* say about where they got their boldness from? They were filled with the Holy Spirit. So you need to be filled with the Holy Spirit and spend time with Jesus *(verse13)*. Then one of the fruits of that will be that you will become bold. Come on let's go.

*Beck-* OK. The End.

You too, like Beck, may feel quite scared at the thought of sharing your faith with strangers, work colleagues, friends or family members, but obedience to God, not the fear of man, needs to be a priority. As you read the pages of this book may you be equipped, blessed and encouraged to step out of the boat (your comfort zone) and share the Gospel wherever you go.

NB. This book has a lot of sub headings, so if like me, you are very busy, and you don't have time to read the whole book but you want to learn how to preach the Gospel quickly, you can skip the testimonies and real life stories and just read the teaching to learn faster. But I do hope you'll read the entire book at some time as the true stories and testimonies are powerful and encouraging. It's the stories that illustrate how the evangelism works in real life.

Names and locations have all been changed for privacy.

*"For I delivered to you first of all that which I also received: that Christ died for our sins according to the Scriptures, and that He was buried, and that He rose again the third day according to the Scriptures,"*

1 Corinthians 15:3-4

*"Desire that your life count for something great! Long for your life to have eternal significance. Want this! Don't coast through life without a passion."*

John Piper

## Chapter 1

# My Journey into Evangelism

## A Walk of Faith

In mid-2008, my sister told me of a DVD series she hadwatched called, 'Way of the Master', by Ray Comfort. She really thought our family should watch it, so we decided to order it. Our entire family watched it as all nine of our children were still living at home at the time. This teaching series had such a big impact on our family. We learnt how to share the Gospel and how to navigate through a conversation. It was a turning point in our family. Our son, Matthew, was at college at the time and suddenly it was like the college became his mission field andhe started sharing the Gospel with all kinds of people on a regular basis. It was encouraging to hear his encounters when he came home each night. David and I also started intentionally looking out for people to share the Gospel with. David's initial 'fishing ground' was McDonald's in Rosny and my fishing ground was Eastlands Shopping Centre.

The Bible talks about Christians being fishers of men, so that's what we started doing. We learnt as we went along. We found some people were willing to listen and others who didn't want to know anything about the Good News. There's nothing like hands-on experience to grow in the ability to share the Gospel. Until then, we really didn't know how to go about sharing the Gospel on a regular basis even though we had led a small handful of people to the Lord over the years.

## Stories from Those Early Years

I got to know Mildred, one of the shop keepers in one of the ladies clothes shops. She was about 10 years older than me. I shared the Gospel with her and then one day we went out for lunch. I gave her a Bible, which she happily accepted. She also came for dinner at our home and I also went to visit her at her home. Through relationship, trust was built and I spent a lot of our time together sharing the Gospel. One funny incident was when I prayed for her at her work. On this particular day Mildred had a swollen ankle and was unable to walk properly. There was nobody else in the shop at the time so I asked if I could kneel down and lay hands on her ankle and pray for healing. I explained the Bible says to lay hands on the sick and they will recover. Well, she agreed. So I got down on my knees behind the counter, laid hands on her ankle and prayed. I was then back up on my feet just as someone walked into the shop.

Another day I was shopping with my four youngest children who were between the ages of about 3 to 10 years old at the time. We went into a men's shop to look for a shirt for David. When we went up to the counter to buy the shirt, one of the shop assistants commented on the good behaviour of my children. I told her they were home-schooled and as we got talking the two other shop assistants joined in. Then one of them asked me what was my secret to life? I said, "You really want to know? It's because we're Christians and we walk with Jesus." She replied, "That explains it!" I then shared the Gospel with the three of them.

## Don't Wait, Just 'GO!'

Oftentimes Christians think they're to wait until someone asks them what that light is in their eye, or what's different about them, but the previous story is the only time I've been asked anything like that. I would have missed out on thousands of opportunities to share the Gospel if I just waited for people to ask me what makes me different. Jesus didn't say wait for the lost to ask. He said to, "GO into all the world and preach the Gospel." We need to be proactive and willing to turn any conversation into the things of God.

## Ben and Judy Armacost

A couple of years after this I met Ben and Judy Armacost. I had heard quite a lot about them and their heart for evangelism and I was delighted to finally meet them. I remember well my first meeting with them. After talking with Ben for a few minutes he said to me he'd like to fan the flame of evangelism in me as he knew I wouldn't fit the box of a lot of churches. He was right. Ben and Judy were such an encouragement to us during those days and the café years. Also when we started the church they came every Sunday that they were in town, just to support and encourage us. Sadly for us, they moved overseas during the second year of the café but we will be forever thankful for their love and support and for their leading by example in evangelism. It was also Ben that introduced me to the EvangeCube (this will be explained later) which has become such a valuable tool for me as I share the Gospel.

## The lead up to the Rock Café

On 5th July 2010 my daughter Joanne and I were praying and she had a few visions. One of those was a vision of a café and all the tables were being wiped down in preparation for something. We didn't think much about that vision at the time, but when I had the inspiration to run a café the following year I remembered this vision. What wonderful confirmation this was, that the Lord was going before us.

Not long after, I started going on prayer walks around the Hobart CBD every Friday, with either Joanne or a friend, to pray for strategy on how to reach the lost souls of our city. I sensed I should take January 2011 off from any ministry and have a time of prayer and partial fasting. On the 5th January 2011, I had a prophetic dream.

## The Dream

I was at a meeting which was set up like a café. I was talking to a lady when she was introduced to get up and speak. When she got up to the front she looked over at me and pointed her finger and said, "I have never met anyone so heavily pregnant with something of God!"

I knew the dream was from God but I really had no idea what it meant. Towards the middle of the month I battled some depression for quite a few days. During that time my eldest son Sean offered to take me out for lunch and to buy me some new jeans. I was so down I didn't want to go, but after some persuading from him and David I went. It always amazes me how God uses us even when we don't feel up to being used. During our time in town I got to share the Gospel with 6 people! *Evangelism isn't so much about whether you feel like sharing the Gospel, but about being obedient even when you don't feel like sharing!*

The depression lifted and later in the month I was invited to a prayer meeting at the home of some friends. During the night someone mentioned a museum called MONA (Museum of Old and New Art), and that we needed to pray God's fire down on it to destroy it. I'd never heard of MONA until then, but I knew it wasn't right to pray God's fire down on it. I suggested we pray for the people involved and that maybe God had a way that we could counteract what MONA was doing. David Walsh the owner, and his activities at MONA blatantly mock Christ and promote a perversion of sex and death. It is all very contrary to the Bible. But as Jesus said to James and John in *Luke 9* when they wanted to call fire down from Heaven and consume those in the Samaritan village that rejected Him, "the Son of Man did not come to destroy men's lives but to save them." The antidote to MONA and the mockery they were starting to bring into Hobart was not the fire of God but the love of God. So I suggested that God would have a way for His people to be a light shining in Hobart to counteract the darkness being promoted by MONA.

Over the next few days I specifically prayed about what we could do, as Christians, in Hobart, to counteract the works of MONA. I knew it wasn't going to have anything to do with fire. As I drove past the Baha'i temple the next day I saw a sign for a café. I thought if they could run a café, what if some Christians in Hobart got together and ran an outreach café with a specific vision to use the café as a place to share Jesus with the lost?

I mentioned the idea of an outreach café to my family and a handful of friends. Everyone seemed to think it was a good idea, but how could it work? I didn't know many Christians in Hobart. One friend who did know a lot of Christians sent out emails to all the pastors and Christians he knew, but there wasn't much interest. Not one to be put off easily, in faith, we started monthly prayer meetings in our home. We had between 12-20 people attend those meetings. We were a motley crew and anyone looking on would have wondered what an earth we could do with such a small group of diverse people. But God had plans!

What should we call this proposed ministry? A few months earlier Joanne had had a vision of a city and the Lord coming and painting a white love heart around it. I did a painting of that vision with Hobart as the city. As we started praying about a name for the ministry I sensed very strongly that we were to incorporate that painting in the name for the ministry.

A friend had a few suggestions of names but none of them gelled. She then said, "Love Hobart." I knew that was it! I checked with some of the others and as we prayed we all felt that was the right name. We decided we should go ahead and register 'Love Hobart' as the business name. But that night someone rang me to say he'd sensed we were moving too quickly with this and that we should wait longer before doing anything. I prayed and asked the Lord to show me. Did He want us to wait or to keep moving forward and register the business name? That night I had a dream that David and I were in a speed boat on a very long, straight river. We were going so fast we got airborne in the boat. (That was one of the coolest dreams I ever had!)

As we prayed we all sensed that we should keep moving forward. We registered the name 'Love Hobart' with ServiceTas and then we wrote a constitution which was checked by a lawyer before we applied to be a not for profit organisation. Everything just started falling into place and all our applications were approved. Love Hobart Inc. became a reality.

One day I was up the mountain (Mt. Wellington) praying with a friend when I sensed we should get a website up and running. I had no idea how to do HTML programming and I knew it would take a while for me to learn, but if that's what I had to do I would. That evening, out of the blue, my son Matthew offered to do a website for us. What an amazing provision this was!

And that website www.lovehobart.com is still being used today. It's been through quite a few changes over the years to accommodate new and different aspects of the ministry of Love Hobart. Nowadays, it no longer requires HTML so I can update it myself.

In August 2011, David and I went to Melbourne. We were taken out for lunch to a café called 'Lentil as Anything.' There was an honesty box so people just put in what they could afford for food. We thought that was a great concept, and that maybe we could incorporate that idea in how we would run our café. We did decide not to charge for food at the café but also had a box there for people to donate if they wished.

During the 2¼ years that we ran the Rock café we never asked for money or donations from anyone, nor applied for any grants. I had thought I was already walking by faith but God stretched my faith even more during that season! He always provided for us.

Also around this time we saw the Odeon theatre had come up for lease. They were asking $38,000 for the lease of the café and the upstairs room with the kitchen. This was way outside our price range, but I couldn't help thinking this could be the place. The Odeon held a bit of history for us personally as a family and it seemed strange to think of being back there to run a café. I used to clean that café every week for a year or so when my youngest was only 2 years old. She and our other three youngest all used to help.

We had about $5,000 in the bank at this time and I sensed the Holy Spirit saying to wait until we had $20,000 in the bank before applying for a lease. It might as well have been $200,000 as I had no way of personally financing this vision. And was $20,000 going to be enough?

One day a friend came driving up our driveway really fast. She came inside and said the Holy Spirit had been impressing on her to give to Love Hobart. She'd been putting it off but was now under conviction. She wrote us out a cheque for $2,000!

Another lady asked to meet me for lunch one day. During the lunch she handed me an envelope with a $1,000 cash in it. God was surely providing.

Then someone else approached me at church and said that when she and her husband sold their land they wanted to donate some money to the vision for the café.

Little by little money started coming in. By mid-November we had just over $19,000. Someone suggested I put in a lease application for the Odeon then as the total raised was now approaching the target of $20,000, but after praying I sensed we needed to wait. Not long after, the lady from church sold her land and a few days later deposited some money in the account. We sat on $19,500! That same day we were given a gift of money for our family. We set aside ten percent of that for the café and that was $500! So we now had $20,000 exactly in the Love Hobart bank account.

So the next step was to apply for a lease. We applied for 2 years at the Odeon. Our offer was substantially lower than what was being asked by the owners but it was still a huge step of faith for us. We went to see the agent to put in our offer. It was a bit embarrassing because it was so low but we really didn't have the money to offer more. The offer was rejected, but two weeks later, amazingly, it was accepted. So we really were going to be running an outreach café!

We had 2 months free lease to get the premises ready for running a café. It was a very busy time for us all and lots of red tape to walk through with the different council departments. However, on Friday 17th February, 2012 The Rock café opened for its first 12 hour day. The day before opening I rang David and told him I didn't really want to run a café and he replied, "It's a bit late for that." The café and the whole ministry was a big step of faith, I was way out of my comfort zone and although the nerves were there, ultimately I just wanted to be obedient to the Lord. I had, after all, told the Lord I would do anything for Him and this was His doing. So the café began.

## The Beginning of the Rock Café

Our first day dawned. We had no idea what to expect, but we were ready. We opened the doors at 10am and nobody came in. We waited 5 minutes; 10 minute; 20 minutes; and still nobody! But at 10:25pm people started coming in. We were even blessed by a visit from a local politician who came in during her break just to support us. We ended up with about 100 people through the doors that first day.

We soon got into a routine with the café and we had a good team of volunteers to help us. Some weeks were very quiet and other weeks we were very busy, but we learnt to trust God no matter what. Every week there were opportunities to share the Gospel as well as do pastoral work. It was an adventure.

Following are some of my updates I wrote during the café season.

## Love Hobart Update- 6th October 2012

Yesterday we had more non-Christians come to the café than Christians-that's the first time that's happened. The teenage 'Goths' from 2 weeks ago came back. I sat with them and had an awesome talk. They're opening up and asking lots of questions. There were a few other groups that came in and we were able to share the vision of the café and many times I shared the Gospel too. Chris came back with a different friend and he had lots of heavy questions for me. Over dinner time a young mum came in and I shared the Gospel with her. She said she wasn't ready for this but then amidst tears she shared her journey and then afterwards accepted a Bible. We also had a few teams go out on the streets last night to share the Gospel.

## Love Hobart Update- 8th December 2012

What an amazing day at the Rock yesterday! The 'Goths' came back again and I shared with them about our son Brodie's miraculous protection after coming off his motor bike at 80km hour on Wednesday when his accelerator jammed. This opened up talk on Heaven and Hell, life and death, and God's protection of His children. There were more people wanting to come to Bible studies so we started a fifth group this week with different ones leading. About 9pm a new group of four girls, all with brightly coloured hair came in. I had an awesome opportunity to share the Gospel with one of them in particular and I entrust the sown seed to the Lord. After that, a young guy came in, having being spoken to through the street evangelism. A few of us spent 1 1/2 hrs with him sharing the Gospel, praying for healing and encouraging him to search for God. We didn't get home until nearly midnight. It was a long but very rewarding day.

## Love Hobart Update- 20th July 2013

Some days at the Rock are hard going. Yesterday was one of those, but amidst it all we had many opportunities to share the Gospel. Two Asians came to our Bible study group, who are not yet saved. At the end of the study I shared the Gospel with them. There was such an openness there, and they both wanted to go away and think on these things. A group of four teens came in who I'd not met before. I shared the Gospel with them. Their stumbling block was evolution. They could not see creation as being valid. Lucy, a girl in her late teens who's been in a few times, showed up by herself and I spent a lot of time with her sharing the Gospel again and answering questions.

Then there was Sue, who's been into the café a lot. I've also been catching up with her quite often during the week. She is so open to the Gospel, but fear is blocking her coming to Jesus. Yesterday she went and talked to a guy that came into the Rock about Jesus! She'll make an amazing evangelist when she gets saved. Then there's Henry who is 22 years old. He first came to the Rock about a year ago and was found on the streets by one of our team last night. He's moved back home but is still very confused. I shared the Gospel with him and prayed for him and dropped him home after the café closed. He's been fed lies that he'll never amount to anything. So many people to pray for...

## Love Hobart Update- 18th August 2013

Friday at the Rock was full on in many ways. Lucy, who's been in a few times came in just before we opened. She was keen to help in the café. She helped for 4 hours! I then spent some time with her to again share about Jesus. I prayed with her and gave her a Bible. She's really searching. We also have a couple of people on our team who are really getting stirred up to do evangelism. They went onto the streets to share the Gospel quite a few times during the day. One group they brought back to the café: an African guy and a guy from Nepal, both in their mid-teens loved the artwork in the café and that opened up the way for sharing the Gospel as all the artwork has a spiritual theme. They were very open and both took Bibles. Then there was Mel who I gave a Bible to about a month ago. She's been reading through it and is up to Judges. She too is searching for the truth. Ethan, who we first met some months back, came in and helped serve in the café in the afternoon. He's starting to get his life in order having come back to Jesus. There were so many opportunities on the streets last night too. It's wonderful to see God raise up young ones with a passion for the lost togo out and do street ministry.

## Love Hobart Update- 19th October 2013

We shared the Gospel many times yesterday, both in the café and on the streets. We're starting to get back-packers into the café again as the weather warms up. A couple from Belgium were very open to the Gospel and another couple from South Korea also listened intently. Last week Tammy came into the café for the first time. She didn't want to talk.

She came back yesterday and she started opening up to me. She then let me share the Gospel with her and she even asked about church. She said she could feel peace at the café and all her anxiety lifted. Alistair, an older guy, came in three times yesterday. He was lonely but also very open to the Gospel. Michael, a young guy from out of town was looking at the EvangeCube as he waited for his food so I asked if I could show him what it meant. He was very open to the Gospel and I could see God was already on his case. Ben, a regular, brought in a friend called Millie. She was very open to listen and talk about Christianity. There's always lots of pastoral work that goes on at the café too and there's often prayer for healing, provision, relationship issues or any number of other things.

## The End of the Rock Café Draws Near

In December 2013 our 2 year lease for the café finished and we went into monthly lease as per the original lease agreement.

We were invited to apply for a one year lease but after prayer we sensed we were to just keep the monthly lease in place. I felt a bit uneasy about what might happen, but I knew this was the right decision before God.

In January 2014 I was approached by someone from MONA regarding the use of the building for their dark event. The previous year they had leased the other parts of the building that we weren't leasing while they hosted their dark event, but this coming year they wanted the entire building. The outcome? In April we received a letter in the mail from the Real Estate Agents to tell us our lease was being permanently terminated. So MONA got the entire building for their dark event. This was a sad time for us initially as we were disappointed the café was going to be closing and we didn't have enough funds to relocate. But what the enemy means for evil against us, God will use for us if we keep a right heart and attitude. There were the gain-sayers who were whispering behind our backs that we must have done something wrong for God to take the café off us. But little did they know that God had a greater work for us coming up out on the streets of Hobart. Also, we were all so tired from the heavy work load of running a café. The next season God had for us was to be more ministry and less physical work. God always knows what's best.

## Faith

Faith is tested through trials. Our response to trials and tests reveal whether we have faith or not. Faith itself comes from hearing the Word. Tests when embraced in faith, produce patience. However patience isn't an automatic outcome. If during tests there is unbelief, grumbling, discouragement or the like, there is then no evidence that you have grown in patience, but when patience grows it will be a sign of a person who is perfect (mature) and complete, lacking nothing (*James 1:2-4*). When everything is going our way, patience and faith are easy. The real test of faith and patience comes when trials come. This was to be a season of more walking by faith and patience for us.

## The End of the Rock Café- 9th May 2014

We sure went out celebrating at our last night at the Rock. We had a packed café as we shared and gave thanks for all the Lord has done during our 27 months of running the Rock. It was also a blessing to have so many people drop in throughout the day to thank us, encourage us and rejoice with us in what the Lord has done in this season. One of the highlights for me was sharing the Gospel with eleven different people. A group of three young ladies who'd never been in before were sad to hear it was our last day but they were so open to hearing the Gospel and they were very happy to be given a Bible each. A group of three young guys came in and again the openness from them to hearing the Gospel was amazing. They asked quite a few questions too. Another group of four teenage guys who had come in before were happy for me to share the Gospel with them and I offered to catch up with them for coffee sometime if they'd like to talk more. Then there was a guy from Adelaide who came in for coffee. Again he was so open to hear the Gospel and I encouraged him that the greatest thing he could do for his family was to come to Jesus and train up his children in God's ways. He was definitely listening. And the Gospel was shared out on the streets again as well. So this is the end of a season but the small seed of Love Hobart continues.

## What Next?

We didn't know initially what God was requiring of us. However, after prayer we all sensed we should keep the church meeting going. We found a council building just up the road from the café that was available for lease on a Sunday afternoon. We were also invited to be a light shining in the darkness at an event at MONA called the Festival of Freedom of Beliefs and Religions. We decided it was right to attend this as it was in the basement away from the actual museum. Three of our sons-Sean, Matthew and Brodie helped David and me on our stall at various times. There were many other religions represented there along with pagans, witches and atheists etc. There were also two other Christian stalls; the Anglican Church and Grace Church. It was an interesting time and the highlight for me was sharing the Gospel with some of the staff from MONA.

Although we were in a season of having been pruned back and sometimes discouragement seemed near, we could still rejoice in what the Lord was doing. With the closing of the Rock café, it was like the

Lord had given us a little push out of the comforts of a building and now all the ministry, apart from our Sunday meeting, was happening out on the streets of Hobart. In being outside, the opportunities to share the Gospel also multiplied many times more than in the café. We did street ministry every Friday night. A few months later, we started doing Saturday nights as well. This was a big commitment and very tiring, but also very rewarding.

## My Story Continues

The first Friday after the Rock café closed, I was asked to go and preach at a home-group in Sandy Bay. My talk was well received and afterwards we met with others (who had been doing street ministry from the café) at Mures at the wharf. We had chips and prayed together before going out for an hour to do street ministry. I went out with David and we had a good night. I was a bit scared in the initial approach to people even though I'd been doing it for so long at the café and Eastlands, so David mostly took the lead.

## The story of Stavros

The best encounter that night was with Stavros, a bouncer outside one of the pubs in Salamanca. He'd had an Anglican upbringing but wasn't walking with Jesus. He was very open to hear the Gospel and ask questions and it was a great introduction for me to street ministry. Every Friday night we would go past the pub where Stavros worked as a bouncer to see if he was on duty. If he was there we'd often spend 20-30 minutes chatting with him, answering his questions and praying for him. It wasn't long before he was keen for me to meet his wife too. So one night I went for a visit. I spent a couple of hours with this lovely couple and by the end of the evening Stavros asked me to lead him in a prayer of recommitment to the Lord. What a beautiful moment that was. Since that time I've been discipling Stavros and walking with him through some battles to victory. Being a Christian is a journey to maturity as an imitator of Christ and that's where discipleship is needed to encourage, teach, equip, train and even bring correction to young Christians when needed.

## The Following Week

On the second week after the café closed, while we were praying at Mures, I had a strong sense that we were to go to the Bus Mall and that we'd find a guy there with a beanie. So off we went and sure enough there was only one guy in the Bus Mall and he was wearing a beanie. I shared the Gospel with him. At this point I was still very nervous about approaching people and starting the conversation, so David did that. David thought I spoke too much to this guy. Usually he did street ministry from the café with a team member who was happy to just let him take the lead. It was a big adjustment for him to go out with me so he wanted to do the talking with the next person. But after talking for 5 minutes with the next guy we approached, David came to a halt as this guy was quiet and non-communicative. So David whispered for me to take over. From then on David encouraged me to lead as he could see God had gifted me in evangelism. I am very aware that this is a gift, that I could not do it on my own. I'm thankful to the Lord for this gift.

## Street Ministry

We were now doing evening street ministry every Friday and Saturday. First for one hour each night, then for 2 hours and then some nights even longer. Even though it was extremely tiring, I enjoyed it. As time went on it became just our family doing it. They would take in turns coming out with me. They didn't enjoy it as much as I did but they were still willing to come out on the streets. Over the course of many months it was very encouraging to see a shift take place as kids from the streets would walk past me and say, "Hello Helen". There was one girl in particular, Laura, who always said hello, and I sensed a real gentleness in her. As I came to know her and her story more, I so easily could have taken her home with me. One day she said to me, "Helen, if I'd been brought up in a Christian home I think things would have been very different." Yes, they probably would have been. I felt so sad. She was a beautiful young lady but she was caught up in excessive alcohol and drug use.

## Love Hobart Update- October 2014

In mid-October during one weekend alone I shared the Gospel with over 30 people. Even though the café had closed, the ministry grew. Some of the highlights from that weekend were a group of six teenagers in the Mall on Friday night. As I walked through the Mall, one of the group waved to me as I'd shared the Gospel with her before. I went over to them and got to share the Gospel with them all and then they let me pray a blessing on them. Later I talked to two Muslim guys, both in their late 30's, one from Egypt and the other from Palestine.

When I first told them I was a Christian they said they didn't want to talk, but I spent an hour with them as they bombarded me with questions. One of them had been reading the Bible so he was very open to hearing the truth of the Gospel. Saturday night I saw four teens in Franklin Square so I went to talk to them. I shared the Gospel and by the time I'd finished there were 10 of them as their friends kept joining. Some were mocking but I just stood my ground and gently kept sharing the truth. Later that night I passed 3 guys in the Bus Mall, one I'd met before and another with a hoodie I couldn't see properly until he turned round and said, "Hi Helen". I knew him from the Rock. I shared the Gospel with the 3 of them and while sharing, two guys from a group I shared with last week recognised me and came over to say hi and listen in. Then Sunday afternoon before church I did some chalk art in Mathers Lane and three teens came and sat on the grass. I finished my picture and got talking to them. Using my EvangeCube I shared the Gospel. They invited 3 girls on the other side of the grass area to come and listen too. These kids were the most open I've ever seen. One of them especially knew he needed to get his life in order and it would require change. I prayed with them all and trust that as seeds are sown God will bring the change.

## Love Hobart Update- 8th December 2014

It was a cold weekend out on the streets of Hobart and subsequently not many people around. But we still had some awesome opportunities to share the Gospel. The highlight for me on Friday night was when two teens approached me while I was sharing with a French backpacker. I'd met one of the teens before and shared Jesus with him. He said he saw me and thought he'd come over and say hi and introduce me to his friend. I shared the Gospel with his friend and they both bombarded me with lots of questions.

On Saturday night it was even quieter than Friday night but I still shared the Gospel a few times. The best part for me was talking to two bouncers outside one of the pubs in Salamanca. I'd shared the Gospel with one of them before but the other one I had never met. I spent about 40 minutes with them and they wanted to know everything from healing and deliverance, to why Lucifer was kicked out of Heaven. So we keep sowing and praying, and waiting for a move of God's Spirit in Hobart.

Yesterday, before our church meeting, I arrived to find the black board had been wiped clean, all ready for a Christmas picture. Even as I was doing the chalk art I was able to share the Gospel with two teens who sat nearby watching me as they chatted. These two had both had Catholic schooling and believed there was a God, so that made for aneasier conversation. I left them with the question, "If you were to die tonight, in light of what I have said, would you go to Heaven or Hell?" I often ask people this question and it's interesting to see the penny drop for many of them as they realise they can't get to Heaven through their own goodness and they need a Saviour, Jesus. What a message of hope we have for this lost and dying world.

## Love Hobart Update-17th January 2015

Love Hobart started off the year with a week of prayer and fasting. We met every evening in Franklin Square to pray. It was great to have people from other ministries join us too, as we prayed for our city and for an outpouring of God's Spirit. Friday night during the prayer meeting there was a streaker in the fountain area of the park: not very nice but a real wake up call to the depravity of human nature and the need for the Gospel to be shared. After the prayer meeting last night we were back into street evangelism after having a break for a month. Having had an eventful week of opposition from the enemy's camp we weren't sure what to expect but the Lord showed Himself faithful to each of the teams out sharing the Gospel. My team shared with a couple on their honeymoon from Bombay. She was a Catholic and he was an agnostic. They listened attentively and let me pray for them. There was another couple from the Philippines who were Catholic who understood the power of the cross and were keen to support what we do through prayer. Another young lady had heard the Gospel from one of our teams a few weeks ago but was eager to hear it again. Then there was Dan, a 15 year old, and his friend, Joe. Dan had no idea who Jesus was but he listened intently to the Gospel. I offered to pray a blessing on him but he said he was too scared. Tonight we went out again, and again we saw God's faithfulness with some very open young people. The highlight for me was Chris who we first met at the Rock 2 1/2 years ago. He came up to me while I was sharing the Gospel with someone and gave me a hug. He waited at a discreet distance until I'd finished. Then I sat on the pavement with him and we had a lovely chat before I prayed for him.

Then off to Salamanca to disciple Stavros. I think our Church and ministry is really about being on the streets.

## The Story Continues

By May 2015 I was starting to get to know a few young people from my consistency of being out on the streets. One of the girls, Laura, really warmed to me. One day I suggested to her that the coming Friday we should meet at Subway for food and God-talk. She came with three friends. I had met two of her friends before but they had been quite rude to me. Now they were a bit coy and later one of them apologised for her earlier treatment of me via one of my daughters.

The following Friday those three came back with three more teens. What an encouragement! I also had five of my kids with me which meant we could talk individually to these teens as well as in a group. I shared the Gospel with the EvangeCube again and then the next 2 hours were spent answering questions, telling them the story of Jonah and talking about everything from abortion to sexual immorality to modesty and God's love. There were also another 8-10 teens that joined in at various times during that 2 hours. We got to pray for some of them and two of them wanted prayer to stop smoking— they're both 14 years old. It was freezing cold that night but we were blessed to run this 'Youth ministry' in the Mall. We gave out more Bibles and Action Bibles which really go down well with these teens. One of them sent me a Facebook message later saying, "Hey Helen thanks for the Bible it means a lot.

God bless ya. You're a pretty helpful person. Thanks again."

Another two of the kids came to church yesterday. It was the first time in a church for them. They really liked it and want to come back. On the Saturday night it was even colder than Friday and the CBD seemed deserted but I found about 10 people to talk to and gave out all my Bibles again! One girl I'd shared the Gospel with a couple of weeks ago saw me and came to tell me she'd been reading her Bible. How exciting! I finished off the night sharing the Gospel with a Pakistani Muslim security guard in Salamanca who wanted a Bible and who happily let me pray for him.

The following Friday there were about 20 kids waiting for me outside Subway for food and God-talk! I thought there's no way I'm going to be able to keep this up. I'd already talked to my small team of helpers at Love Hobart and asked if they'd be willing to help me run a Youth night on Friday nights when the need arose. It became obvious that we needed to start Youth.

## Youth Night Starts

The next Friday we started Youth night. We had no idea what to expect. I'd caught up with the Police Inspector in the week to let him know of my intention. He warned me it could be a difficult task but also encouraged me that he thought I had the strength to do it, no matter what it looked like.

So how did the first Youth night go? Nothing at all like we expected. It was like Satan was trying to rail road us. I went to meet the kids outside Subway as previously arranged to then walk with them to Youth. When I arrived at Subway there was a handful of kids there but one girl, Hayley, was 'off her face' drunk! She started vomiting everywhere. Some of the kids still wanted to come to Youth so I said I'd take them and show them where it was then I'd come back to help Hayley and her two friends who stayed with her. In the few minutes that I was gone Hayley started having seizures and her friends called an ambulance. The paramedics came and put her on a stretcher and took her to the hospital. Her two friends then came back with me to Youth but of course we were all concerned for Hayley. Half a dozen of us walked up to the ER to see if we could find out how Hayley was. No news. We went back to Youth and then back to the hospital again. Hayley's Mum came not long after and Hayley had sobered up a lot so her Mum took her home. I will add that Hayley has come a long way since that night. She is a beautiful young lady with a beautiful heart.

## The Second Youth Night

The following Friday no one came to Youth. That was disappointing but we were being available for God. I went and did some street ministry while the others were on standby at Youth. A handful of youth came the following week and then none the week after. But things were about to change. We then started getting 20-30 kids each week but half of them would either be drunk or high on weed. This meant there was potential for fights and aggravation as different groups of kids didn't get on with each other and when drugs and alcohol were involved it was full on. A couple of times I nearly called for police assistance but each time the near-fight would stop.

## Love Hobart Update- 22nd June 2015

It was an exhausting, blessed, fruitful, chilly and wet, 10 nights on the streets doing evangelism, sharing the Gospel with 100+ people while

MONA had their dark event in the city. On a few of the nights I took out new people with me to train in evangelism. Some highlights: my 15 year old daughter Emily was asked by some 17 year olds why she believed in Jesus and so in less than 1 minute she shared the Gospel. I think the 2 girls were quite amazed! One night I saw five teens jay-walking in front of me. We waited for the green man but caught up to this group in the Mall. I shared the Gospel with three of this group who all listened intently and happily took Bibles. One night a couple of drunks (50-year-olds) approached me. So I shared the Gospel with them and offered to pray. They were very moved that I would pray for them. There were many others: atheists, Buddhists, tourists, medical students, college students, high school students, Catholics and some who think they're Christians but it's obvious when talking with them they have no concept of repentance, the power of the cross or living a holy life with Jesus as Lord. Sometimes it feels overwhelming to talk with so many people who are lost and facing an eternity in Hell. But we press on and pray and preach the Gospel.

Yesterday four young people from street ministry came to church, two of them were 15 year old guys who had never been to a church before. They said they'd be back, and they have been. I've got to know these two quite well and I'm now on Facebook with them and many kids I've met on the streets.

## Bible Study in Subway

On one Tuesday afternoon in late July, I ended up doing an impromptu Bible study in Subway with four teens: all non- Christians that I'd met through the street ministry! It was very interesting, especially when one went off to buy a bong in the middle of the study! At the end of the study they allowed me to pray for them and three of them put their hands together in a praying position. There was no fear about what anyone thought about them. The Bible study I did was on forgiveness. I had opportunity to put what I taught these teens into practice the following Friday night.

## The Stolen Phone

It was around the eighth week since we had started Youth and we had about 25 youth that night which was great. I was sitting talking to a group of girls, then I moved to talk to some others. A couple of minutes later, I noticed my phone was no longer in my back pocket. I went back to where I has been sitting but it wasn't there. One of the girls said she'd seen it on the chair but it wasn't there now. It was gone. It had fallen out of my pocket onto the chair and now one of the kids had stolen it! My heart sank as I felt my privacy had been violated. I wasn't angry but it was such a disappointment.

What happened next was very interesting. As soon as word got out that my phone was stolen there was quite an uproar. Some of the kids who had gotten to know me well were very angry that someone would steal my phone after all I did for them (their words). Some asked if I'd stop doing Youth because of it and I said, "Of course not." A couple of the guys had their skateboards under their arms and said they were going to hit the person on the head with their skateboards when they found the thief. I talked to them about not retaliating and that we need to pray for those who curse us. They thought I couldn't be serious but they could see I wasn't angry. Of course I wasn't happy my phone was stolen but there's a God-way to respond to these things which I endeavoured to show these kids.

## The Following Day

The following day I went out late in the afternoon to do street ministry. I talked to a lot of people, some whom I already knew. At one point a girl came running up to me calling out, "Helen, my hand got healed after you prayed the other week". I'd only met her that once, so that was very encouraging to hear. Later I introduced myself to a young guy, Aiden. A couple of kids from Friday night came along asking me if my phone had shown up and I chatted to them for a while. Aiden listened in on the conversation and I said to him, "You can see I really am out on the streets a lot." That opened the way for me to share the Gospel. He happily received a Bible and I prayed with him. I also talked with a security guard in town, then a guy who was around 30-years-old who had been abused by a 'Christian' relative when he was young. This had obviously turned him off Christianity. I explained to him that the man was probably not a Christian as he would not have done that if he really was. He agreed and said that guy was now old and bitter and didn't believe in God any more.

## Love Hobart Update- 24th August 2015

What an exciting week! On Tuesday I bumped into Chris who I first met 3 years ago at the Rock who used to dress as a girl.

He's now very much a young man and we had an awesome catch-up for an hour over coffee. Sadly he's been badly judged at times by some Christians but his heart is very soft towards us and the Gospel. We have loved him, fed him and accepted him wherever he was at. Well a big surprise yesterday he showed up at church and then came out for dinner with us. On Friday night I arrived 20 minutes early at Youth and there were two of the girls waiting for me. They wanted to do street evangelism with me (they're not Christians yet), so off we went and shared the Gospel before I was messaged to get back to Youth because there were heaps of kids there. That night 25- 30 kids came through and everyone stayed longer and were more interested in talking than playing pool etc. When I arrived at Youth one kid came straight up to me to apologize. I asked, "For slapping me in the face?" He said, "You remembered?" To which I responded, "Well I never got slapped in the face before!" He was in the Mall and very drunk when that happened last weekend. I told him I forgave him and gave him a hug. He was taken aback. Later I shared the Bible story of Joseph with a couple of other teens; prayed for different ones and had a long talk with a guy about 'God-stuff'. When I prayed for him he started crying as the Spirit of God touched him.

Another teen said to me, "Joe has given up drinking and actually Helen, everyone is changing!"

I knew about Joe as he was coming to church every week and even his school teachers were amazed at the change. Another girl who was an atheist when I first met her told me on Friday she has now decided to go to a Christian college next year. But the big highlight for me was when Tim walked in. He has followed me around on the streets at times saying, 'f* this', and 'f* that', while telling people not to listen to me or yelling at me to go away. He came straight up to me and said, "Helen, I'm sorry for being so mean to you". I told him I forgave him. We had a good chat and we're now friends on Facebook. Two apologies in one night! And that's just Friday night.

Then there was Saturday street ministry. Some highlights: a lady, around 40 years old was sitting outside Target feeling sick and rundown. I shared the Gospel with her and prayed for healing. An older couple from South Australia just wanted to talk about this and that to start with, but perseverance paid off and I was able to share about why Jesus died on the cross for our sins. Then I talked to three young teens who all said they were Christians but were regularly looking at pornography and participating in other sins. I challenged them to get right with God and flee the lusts of the flesh. A young guy who lives in a shelter seemed a bit spaced out but I shared Jesus, gave him a Bible and prayed with him. Later I talked with two late-teens who had just finished work: one was open, the other one wasn't. As I gently talked and shared the Gospel they both softened and both took Bibles and let me pray for them. It's been a full on weekend, I get so excited sometimes I take a while to wind down and sleep at night.

## Love Hobart Update- 31st August 2015

I often ask the kids I've got to know well, what would be the one thing that would stop them from becoming a Christian? Their answers are different and varied. The funniest one was 'other Christians!' Mostly it's the alcohol. Joe loves his rap music and said that would be a block for him, so I bought him two Christian rap CD's this week which he said were ok but he preferred his music which he said is pretty special to him. I replied, "Jesus is pretty special". His reply, "Jesus is very special". On Wednesday I took Matt to his drug and alcohol rehab appointment. We had lunch together after and then he wanted me to meet his Mum who he hadn't seen for a couple of months. So I took him to his Mum's and we spent some time there. She is a Christian, so was very happy to know I'd been helping her son out. He and his friend had both been drug and alcohol free for over a month. On Thursday we took Matt and Joe with us to watch 'War Room', a Christian movie, and thankfully they were really well behaved. At Youth the next night they were talking about how much they'd enjoyed it. We also got some artwork happening at Youth with a couple of the kids. About 25 kids came through with 3 new ones who came in with their friends. There were many opportunities to share testimonies, Bible stories and pray. Saturday afternoon was very cold (it has been the coldest winter in Hobart in 50 years!) but we found 17 people out on the streets to share the Gospel with, giving out more Bibles and praying for many. The best part of the week was after I finished preaching on Sunday. Chris came up to me and whispered he'd like to say something after the last song. Well he's not saved yet and I'm thinking to myself what is he going to say? So I just asked him if it was good. "Yes Helen", he replied. So I handed the mike over to him when the song ended and Chris, a bit nervous got up and spoke. He took my breath away by honouring me and my family for all we've done for him and the other youth in Hobart, commending us for our love and how non-judgemental we were, especially toward him when he used to dress as a girl and do drugs. He thanked us for feeding him and loving him when he was hungry, homeless and alone. I just give praise to the Lord for all He is doing in Hobart in these precious young people, one by one by one.

## Love Hobart Update- 7th September 2015

All kinds of things happened this week including six new kids that came to Youth with their friends. Only a couple were stoned and the others I shared the Gospel with and gave out some Bibles. It's a good sign when the kids we know are bringing their friends to Youth. On Saturday afternoon in the Mall we saw a couple of the girls we knew who were stoned. They were quite rude to us but one of them sent a message later apologising. We shared the Gospel with a Filipino Catholic lady who was not walking with Jesus. We prayed with her. We took three kids to McDonald's for dinner and my daughter Emily went through the EvangeCube with them for her first time. She did well. There was a group of four older teens in Franklin Square and we had a full-on talk about all kinds of things. They wanted to know why God allows suffering. We also discussed creation versus evolution, aliens and demons and many other topics. At the end they let me pray with them and they were happy with our discussion. One of them actually showed up at church yesterday along with six other kids from street ministry. They were very attentive to the sermon and most of them stayed after church for coffee and chats. Another seven kids showed up after church finished of which two were stoned, and one of those had been hallucinating. He wanted prayer but he was very anxious and didn't want me to leave him. He just needed a lot of reassurance, more prayer, food and water and the side effects of the weed subsided. Quite a few of the kids came and had dinner with us after. Unbeknown to me, after I left church a mini fight broke out between two groups. Thankfully everyone was ok. These kids need lots of prayer and we need continued patience, bucket loads of love and much wisdom. Doing ministry has its challenges but there's much to be thankful for too.

## Love Hobart Update- 21st September 2015

On Friday night we had 30+ kids come to Youth. It was intense at one point as some of them were quite drunk when they arrived. There was a fair bit of yelling outside as there were issues with breakups in relationships. One of the girls who was very aggravated let me bring her inside and pray with her. All the drunk ones then left to catch a bus to go to a party but Hayley got left behind in town. I received a phone call from those on the bus asking if I could go and look for Hayley, as she had no phone on her. We found her in the Mall, quite distressed, with no money and no friends around. She was thirsty so I gave her my water, she had no money so I gave her bus fare and then we sat with her at the bus stop until her bus came. We returned to Youth and later 2 boys who we hadn't seen for a few weeks came by. They thanked me for praying with them before they left last time. They said that meant a lot. Joanne did a Bible story with a couple of kids. We also get kids from many different countries coming to Youth. This Friday, two new ones came from Afghanistan and two from Iraq. They had Muslim backgrounds, but one was very open to the Gospel.

I did 3 hours of street ministry on Saturday afternoon, and the Gospel was shared with 20+ people. There was also 'God-talk', prayers and hugs with kids who I know, including some who were in the arguments on Friday night. Life is full on and I never know what to expect next but this I do know: God is in charge and He is going before me on this crazy journey and He is moving in the hearts of these kids. So we press on in faith, love, and patience while being the hands and feet of Jesus to these young ones.

## Love Hobart Update- 6th October 2015

We are being stretched with the unexpected! Friday night nobody came to Youth, but our son Joseph (12) said, "It's early, they just haven't come yet." Sure enough around 8pm a dozen kids trickled in. One was new, 15 years old and homeless. I shared the Gospel with him and fed him of course. I talked and prayed with some of the others. They are also getting more comfortable around my kids as everyone is getting to know each other.

Saturday was busy with lots of people to talk to. A couple of 15 year olds from Queenstown were very open and took a Bible and I prayed for them. At a bus stop there were five young guys who were very polite and had lots of questions about Jesus. Most of them took Bibles. Also we saw a few kids I knew from the café so we talked with them and many others. Then on Sunday at 3:55pm, six kids rocked up to church with Joe. As we normally have communion at 4pm (before church at 4:30pm) we decided to do a mini-church for 10 minutes instead of communion. So I shared a couple of Bible stories, Joanne shared a testimony, David prayed and then I finished off with the Gospel. Then food! They left to catch a bus at 4:30pm while we then started our regular church meeting. During the sermon three of the Africans came in too.

Its hard work out on the streets, and it's sometimes discouraging, but when we feel low it's amazing how God will do something extra special just to encourage us like our unplanned pre-church service with those seven kids.

## Love Hobart Update- 9th November 2015

A heap of kids showed up on Friday at Youth and enjoyed pizza. There were three guys (two who I'd met before) sitting around the side of the building, so I went outside and shared the Gospel with them and then we chatted about all kinds of things to do with the Christian life. They willingly took Bibles and let me pray with them. These guys later decided to come into Youth. Around the front of the building were three more guys who I'd never met before. More 'God-talk' and sharing the Gospel and they came into Youth too. Some of the girls showed up later in the evening, a bit drunk, and one of them wanted prayer. After I prayed for her, she prayed for me. This was the first time she'd prayed out loud with anyone. On Saturday I went to her home and did a Bible study with her and afterwards had a chat with her Dad. She then came and helped for a while with the free sausage sizzle we had on in the park. Although it was quite cold at the sausage sizzle we got talking to all kinds of people, from wealthy tourists from all different places, to homeless teens, to drunks and lonely adults. Some even stayed to help us pack up.

On Sunday, three kids from street ministry came to church again and one answered the question, "What do you have to do to be saved?" His answer, "give up a lot of stuff!"

Before our prayer meeting on Monday night I was invited to sit down with a few kids I knew in the park. Jane, who I first met on Saturday, is 18 and homeless. She was excited to share a 'God-dream' she'd had. She's been asking God to speak to her since I met her and she seems to be understanding what Christianity is about.

## Where Are We Now?

## Learning Their Language

I've learnt about words like 'bong' and 'goon bag' which I'd never heard of before. I've had kids ask if they could teach me to smoke when they find out I've never smoked. I've had older young people offer to take me to a nightclub when they found out I've never been to one. But to all these things I reply, "No thank you." I explain I have something better. It's not so much that these young ones want to lead me into sin, but that they think what they are doing is fun. So it's really a sign of acceptance that they want to include me in what they're doing.

## 'God-Talk' Culture

Over time I've been able to establish a discipleship culture amongst these precious young people. They may not be saved yet but when we go out for wedges and 'God-talk' I'm establishing a culture of prioritising talk on the things of God. 'God-talk' may include questions and answers on Christianity, Bible stories or testimonies, teaching on forgiveness or what it means to be holy. It seems we're doing things back to front as we disciple the lost, but that's how it's working out for us. At the end of our time at a coffee shop one of the kids will invariably say, "We need to go now but Helen's got to pray for us first." What an encouragement that is. Then I ask each one what they need prayer for and then I pray, usually with my eyes open so nobody feels embarrassed about being prayed for in a public place. Then they get up to leave, and one by one they give me a hug and off they go till next time.

## Food and 'God-Talk'

I always feed the kids when they're hungry. Sometimes the kids will come find me because they are hungry and other times I'll get a text, "Helen are you in town? Can we go out for wedges and 'God-talk'?" Am I being used? Well if I am, isn't that really a good thing as these kids are being fed physically and spiritually. Isn't that the exact same thing Jesus did? He fed the hungry. Sometimes kids will come to me and tell me so and so is using you, but I just tell them that's ok. I think I'm just showing them what Jesus would do.

A lot of the time though, the kids will actually say to me, "Helen, you don't have to waste your money on us, we're ok." And to that I reply, "I'm not wasting my money; you're worth it." Sometimes they're in the park and the wind is hurling and the rain is coming down and they'll initially be hesitant tocome as they don't want me spending too much money on them. But I reassure them that it's ok and then off we go to a coffee shop.

We are now in 2017 and the ministry of Love Hobart is alive and well. I continue to do street ministry a couple of days a week. Of course, there's always other opportunities before or after church, at prayer meeting and Youth, or really any time I go out. Youth night is usually a lot easier now than the early days. We rarely get anyone coming drunk or high on weed anymore and over time we have seen the trust and respect grow. We get our regulars coming every week and even if they have a party or something else, they'll come by Youth for a bit first. We would love to see many salvations but that's not happening yet, but we are praying over the seeds sown. More about that in Chapter 6.

## Love Hobart Update- 27th March 2017

I spoke to a lovely 82 year old Jewish lady from Melbourne. She did not believe Jesus was the Son of God, but twice she said she envied me that I did believe. I saw Luke with Jack and his brother. We ended up at a café and I went through the EvangeCube. They asked me if tattoos would stop them going to Heaven. Rather than get into the issues of tattoos with them, I answered by asking if they'd ever lied. Of course they admitted they had. I said that lying will stop you going to Heaven.

On Friday I again bumped into Jack and Luke and their friend Reece and then Luke's older sister. Jack really wanted me to put him in this book so I've added his story. Later that day I saw Mark who I met about 8 months ago. He is a male in his mid-twenties who is in the process of becoming a female. I remembered his name and went up to talk. He was happy to see me this time (last time he was very guarded with me although he had tears in his eyes when I prayed). We had a lovely chat and I assured him that God loves him. When we finished talking I put out my hand to shake his and he bentover and gave me a huge hug. A lot of these kids need unconditional love from us while we stand on the truth of the Word. He knows we disagree on some things but I still love him as a person made in the image of God.

As I walked to Youth there was a group of five late-teenssitting on the grass. I'd not met any of them before. They didn't know there was a Youth night nearby. I spent 1/2 hr or so talking with them, sharing the Gospel, answering questions and a few of them took Bibles. Later I took out muffins and there was another group of four who I didn't know and they all came into Youth. Then Anna who I first met 2 1/2 yrs ago on the streets showed up with two friends.

On Sunday before church, Brock was sitting outside on the grass. He's 19 years old and homeless at the moment. He had all his belongings with him including his Bible. We talked and I prayed for him. I invited him in but he didn't come.

After church a 24 year old girl came in to use the toilet. She then brought her partner in. I shared the Gospel. They then let me pray for them. She started crying as the Holy Spirit touched her. I went and got Bibles for them and she said to her partner, "Did you feel that?" He didn't, but she had sensed God. We always need to be ready, willing, and available to share the hope that is within us even when we're tired, and don't feel like it.

## Story of James

Early in 2016, James came to Youth night with Riley, for the first time. As we talked, I found him to be quite arrogant. We didn't see him then until much later in the year when he showed up at Youth night again with Riley. We had a discussion that night that we had different opinions on and I really didn't think we'd see James again.

In February 2017 James showed up at Church on the Rock for the first time with three others who were all connected to a shelter for young guys. James came up to me after church and said how much he enjoyed the service and that he'd be back. We didn't see him for quite a few weeks though.

In late March, Riley decided to leave Hobart for the mainland. He came to visit us at church on the Sunday prior to his departure and when we heard that his flight was early on Wednesday morning we offered for him to sleep over on Tuesday night as we live near the airport. When I met him in town on Tuesday afternoon to bring him back for dinner, James was with him. I invited James for dinner too and offered to drop him back into town after. James really didn't want us to go out of our way for him, but he was very keen to spend a bit of extra time with Riley, so he came. The guys did a Bible study together and then we all prayed for Riley. Somehow James lost his phone during the evening. He'd been outside to smoke quite a few times, but being dark it was more difficult to look for a phone. James left without his phone but we assured him we would look for it in the next day. We couldn't find it.

On the Saturday evening I had a Facebook message from James asking me to remind him what time church was on. He showed up at church with Ben who has only been a Christian for a short time. After church James happily told us he had recommitted his life to Jesus while at home on Saturday night. That was so encouraging to hear and see, as James even looked different.

He had humbled himself under God's hand and become a child of God. The change was very noticeable.

James came for dinner again the following Tuesday with the intention to have one last look for his phone. God used the lost phone to get James to our home again and I was able to pray for him specifically regarding deliverance from addictions.

James found giving up weed and drunkenness relatively easy but he also wanted to give up cigarettes. That was a bit more challenging. He got a prescription medication called 'Champix' to help, and along with prayer and God's help he remains clean of cigarettes, although there has been temptation at times. This is a huge victory, but it can still be a daily struggle.

A couple of weeks later on Good Friday James asked me a lot of questions about baptism. He has such a passion to be right with God and learn as much as he can. I had the awesome privilege of baptising him in our Jacuzzi on Easter Saturday.

Then to top all that off, James has a deep desire to share the Gospel with the lost. This is so encouraging to me personally as now he is coming out on the streets of Hobart with me as I train him in evangelism. This all reminds me of what happened in the book of Acts when people were saved and that excites me. It's been a long, slow road at times, but it's so worth the cost when I see how God has transformed James and others.

*"… the righteous are bold as a lion."*

*Proverbs 28:1b*


*"To evangelise is to spread the Good news that Jesus Christ died for our sins and was raised from the dead according to the Scriptures, and that as the reigning Lord He now offers the forgiveness of sins and the liberating gift of the Spirit to all who repent and believe."*

*John Stott*

*Chapter 2*

# Fearless Evangelism
## What? Me! GO?

S ome people think I'm very brave to go up and talk to strangers. Well to be honest, it still can be a bit daunting at times. I sometimes get asked, "Is it dangerous?" Of course there's always a measure of danger in being out and about on the streets talking to strangers. But having talked to thousands of people I've really had very little trouble, maybe a handful of people at the most, and of those only two that were very full-on, verbally aggressive. That's a very small percentage in light of the number of people I've talked to. I've also seen God's protection from trouble.

One Saturday night there were two teams that met in the Bus Mall. After some time praying, one team headed for Salamanca and my team felt led to go to the hospital. About half an hour later we came back through the Bus Mall and there were police and police cars everywhere. Whatever had happened, the Lord had seen to it that we were right out of the way and protected.

## It Could Be Dangerous!

We are to preach and teach the Word at all times, no matter the cost. We only have to look at the book of Acts to see the cost of preaching the Word. The Apostles were beaten and imprisoned. Stephen was martyred but many people were saved. There were, and still are, always two different results from the preaching of the cross. Some accept the message and some reject it. This rejection was the start of persecution for the early church. Wherever God moves mightily, Satan shows up to oppose God's work and to try and silence those involved. Satan will often use religious people to do his work. But no matter what, those first Christians kept preaching. There was a cost, but that never stopped them. When the apostles were released from prison they rejoiced that they had been counted worthy to suffer for Christ's sake. The Word says,

*"The angel of the Lord encamps all around those who fear Him, and delivers them."*

*Psalm 34:7*

*"Whenever I am afraid, I will trust in You." Psalm 56:3*

In *Acts 5:28* the disciples were told not to teach in Jesus' name, but they replied they ought to obey God rather than man *(verse 29)*. In *verse 16*, they healed and set many free from unclean spirits, in fact all who came to them. But for that, they were persecuted. Their response was always to keep preaching Jesus.

As week after week the Gospel is going out on the streets of Hobart, we are having an impact in the spiritual realm. We may not always be aware of the spirit realm but there will be times when we are opposed in various ways. We must remember we have the Lord God Almighty on our side and we have the Holy Spirit who is given to those who obey Him. Daily we need to continue preaching and teaching Christ and walk in obedience by the leading of the Holy Spirit. Then we will see a shift in the Heavenly places and an outpouring of the Holy Spirit.

Remember the Gospel message is a gift, a precious treasure from the Lord, for us to share with this lost generation. Who will you share this precious, priceless gift with today? Don't be afraid for the Lord goes before you. It is His desire that none should perish *(1 Timothy 2:3-4; 2 Peter 3:9).*

## Testimony of God's Protection

One day I was in the park talking to a group of young people. There were maybe fifteen young people around, and I knew about ten of them. I was talking to about four of them, when a middle aged lady came along the path. I knew her because once before she had verbally threatened me. She was an alcoholic. She saw me, and initially ignored me and went to walk on. She then turned towards me and said, "Hello Helen". It looked like she was going to just go on her way but then she decided to come right round in front of me. She started suggesting I was into all kinds of sin and she then told the kids I'd told her she was worthless and that God didn't care for her. Rocky piped up, "That's not true Helen wouldn't do that." She was right up close as she continued to verbally go off at me, I was quietly praying and asking God what to do. I felt like running, and I felt sick about the whole situation, but I didn't want to leave the kids in a vulnerable situation. I took my phone out of my pocket, ready to call the police as she was getting angry. I was concerned she might try hurting me or one of the kids. Rocky distracted her by talking to her but she continued to falsely accuse me of all kinds of perverted sin. At around this point Lucy came and stood right next to me, shoulder to shoulder, with her arms folded in front of her.

Then Sarah stood on my other side, with her arms folded. Then some guys came and then another and another and they made a wall of protection alongside me and in front of me. While this was going on

Rocky told the lady to leave. He said, "You're lying about Helen. Just get out of here and go!" She argued and there was a bit of talk back and forth but this young guy was persistent, so she started to walk off. As she walked away some of the kids called after her not to come back and to just leave me alone. That was a pretty intense experience but what a blessing to see all those precious young people come to my defence. When I thanked them after, Sarah said, "It's no worries at all Helen. You've done so much for all of us, so it's only fair we return a favour once in a while."

As I walked out of the park after that incident I rang my hubby to tell him what had happened. It was reassuring to hear his voice at the end of the phone. He checked I was Ok. And I replied, "I think so." It wasn't nice what had happened and even though I felt like going home, I went and shared the Gospel with a few more people before leaving town that day.

## Story of Verbal Abuse

On another occasion, I approached a group of four teenage girls in the park; three were friendly, but the other one wasn't. As I started talking with them about my being a pastor the one girl, Stacy started staring at me. She didn't blink at all and I could only describe her look as a death-stare. She didn't say anything but just kept staring. I wasn't sure what to do as I hadn't met anyone like this before. Then suddenly she opened her mouth. She spat out that her Dad was a pastor and she hated God and Christians and she told me to f* off. I didn't try to reason with her. I just blessed everyone and left.

A few months later I shared the Gospel with a teen, Sarah, who was feeling quite down. She was a lovely sweet girl and was very happy to take a Bible and let me pray for her. She told me a friend of hers had a dad who was a pastor and she was actually waiting to meet this friend. Just as I finished praying with her, her friend approached. It was Stacy! On seeing me she glared and then told me in no uncertain terms to f* off and to f* leave her friends alone and to f* get out of there! I got up immediately and said goodbye to Sarah, and blessed them both. As I walked off. I saw a friend of mine up the other end of the Mall so I went and told her what had happened. I also rang my hubby and a friend to ask them to pray for me.

It usually takes me a little while to get over that kind of thing, but I often find the best thing to do is just get right back into sharing the Gospel. Again, not a very nice situation to walk through, but it is sometimes part of the cost of being available for God's work. These are the hardest two people I've met that were really difficult and verbally abusive, so that's such a small percentage in light of the thousands I've talked to.

## Where Do You Get Boldness From?

Let's look at Acts for the answer to that question. In *Acts 3* we read of Peter and John healing a man at the Gate Beautiful, and then they preached Jesus. This preaching, along with the healing that followed, got them into big trouble with the authorities, but not with God. Then in *Acts 4*, Peter and John were arrested as their preaching of Jesus worried the religious leaders. Even though Peter and John were put in custody until the following morning, many still believed—5000, in fact!

The next day they were brought before the authorities. The rulers and elders acknowledged that a notable miracle had taken place *(Acts 4:16)* and demanded to know by what power or what name this had been done. Peter, filled with the Holy Spirit, spoke in the power of God. Peter was bold. This is the same Peter that denied Christ three times. What had changed? He now had the Holy Spirit living in him, having been filled with the Spirit at Pentecost. The Holy Spirit gives power and enables us to be witnesses for Jesus *(Acts 1:8)*. The Holy Spirit will give you boldness to preach about Jesus, just like He gave Peter.

Peter boldly asked why they were even questioning that this good deed had been done. It's not like they had done anything bad; it was a healing followed by Peter preaching Jesus. He boldly declared to the authorities that by the name of Jesus Christ of Nazareth the lame man was made whole. He then said that Jesus had been crucified by them and rejected by them. Peter was very pointed in saying that, but it was the truth. Peter continued by telling them that God raised Jesus from the dead. If Jesus was still dead there would be no power in His name. But He is not dead, He's alive. He is the living Christ and there is still power in His name today because He lives.

Peter declared that there's salvation in no other name than Jesus. You cannot come to the Father any other way. No other prophet or religion can bring you to God the Father—only Jesus Christ, the Son of God. He is the way to God the Father; not Buddha, not Muhammad, not any Hindu god. Only Jesus!

When the authorities saw the boldness of Peter and John they marvelled and were astonished that they were unlearned men, but one observation they made was that Peter and John had spent time with Jesus. They weren't educated as such, but they had been with Jesus. These two men knew Jesus and now they had the Holy Spirit who gave them boldness.

So if you want to get bolder and as a Christian that should be a desire, ask yourself, "Am I spending time with Jesus? Am I reading His Word every day (that's your choice)? Am I worshipping Jesus in Spirit and in truth? And am I filled with the Holy Spirit?"

Also be aware of who you hang out with. Who are you spending time with? Who you spend time with will determine who you become like. Find men and women of God that you can hang out with who can encourage you in God's ways and encourage you to be bold and share the

Gospel. Look at people's fruit. For example, if you want to have a good marriage talk to someone who has a good marriage. That's wisdom! If you want to raise your children in God's ways talk to someone who has done that. That's wisdom! If you want to be bold to share the Gospel hang out with someone who is bold. That's wisdom!

Another interesting note on this event in *Acts 3* and *4* is the evidence of the power of the Name of Jesus. The healed man was standing next to Peter and John and the religious leaders were silenced. This miracle could not be denied. So what could they do? The council conferred together; they wanted to do something to Peter and John even though they hadn't done anything wrong. They couldn't deny the miracle but they were worried that more people would hear and follow Jesus. They decided to caution Peter and John that they were not to speak of Jesus anymore.

Peter and John would not give into intimidation. They answered again, in boldness, in the power of the Spirit, that they could not, they WOULD NOT, stop speaking of Jesus. They would obey God no matter the cost. They were basically saying that these religious leaders were not of God and that they were not hearing God even though they had positions in religious leadership. Peter and John were not afraid to say it as it was: they spoke the truth. They would not obey this command. They could not BUT speak about Jesus.

We either choose NOT to speak about Jesus or we cannot BUT speak about Jesus. There are two options. Either you will NOT speak of Jesus or you cannot BUT speak of Him. Which group do you fall into? There is no middle ground. What are you speaking about? At work? At home? With family? With friends? Can you not help BUT speak about Jesus?

Peter and John had been with Jesus. They couldn't help BUT speak about Him. If you are spending time with Jesus you'll want to talk about Him. We love to talk about what or who interests us. Get close to Jesus.

Hang out with Him and the Holy Spirit will give you boldness to stand up for Jesus in any circumstance.

After the warning, Peter and John were let go as they hadn't broken any law. They'd actually done something very good and even though they would not obey the instructions of the council to keep quiet about Jesus, they were set free as the council was worried of an uprising from the people.

## So What Did Peter and John do?

They went to their own companions and they praised and thanked God together and declared that God would do whatever He determined to be done. So what was the outcome from the threats of the Council? Did Peter and John get scared and stop preaching? No! Did they pray to have their circumstances changed? No! Did they pray for protection? No! They were concerned for the lost and so... they prayed for even more boldness from God *(Acts 4:29)*!! They were already bold but they wanted to be even bolder! Their hearts were to see the message of the Gospel reach as many as possible. This is the heart of the Father, that none should perish *(John 3:17)*.

Peter had a burning desire to preach the Gospel to the lost. When he wasn't preaching he was praying for more boldness to preach more, so more people could hear, because without hearing how could they know Jesus? Will you pray for that kind of passion for the lost? Will you ask God for boldness? Or if you're already bold, will you ask to be bolder?

## Burning House Illustration

Ray Comfort gives an illustration similar to this. If someone was in a burning house and you were there what would you do?

Would you just walk past and keep quiet? No! You'd start knocking on the door and yelling out, "Fire! Fire! Your house is on fire!" How much more then should we warn the lost that there is an eternal fire awaiting them if they will not repent of their sins and accept Jesus Christ as Lord and Saviour. If they choose to ignore the warning it is to their peril, but woe to us if we will not warn them. May it NOT be said of us that people fell into Hell because we failed to warn them.

## Peter and John were Bold

Peter and John would not obey the religious leaders. This test, which the council intended to silence them, fired them up to proclaim the name of Jesus even more. They prayed that they would have more boldness to speak the Word of God and Peter asked God to confirm the Gospel with healings, signs and wonders. They prayed to the God of Heaven for the opposite of what the religious leaders had demanded them to do, and God was on their side. Their prayers were answered immediately. The place where they were literally shook, by the power of God. The infilling of the Holy Spirit caused them to speak the Word of God with boldness. No fear of man here. An evidence someone is filled with the Spirit will be that they cannot BUT speak of Jesus in boldness, no matter the consequences. The Holy Spirit always promotes Jesus Christ the Son of God and the Holy Spirit will always lead us to talk about Jesus.

## Are You Being Bold to Use the Name of Jesus?

Our opponents, Satan and his cohorts, know there is power in the Name of Jesus. Satan and his demons know the power of the Name of Jesus when used by God's people. Today the persecution in the West is somewhat different as now the spotlight is on issues such as abortion, homosexuality, same-sex marriage, transgenderism, sexualisation of children and the like. At this time we are not at high risk of jail for speaking about Jesus, although times are changing fast. Are you using the freedom you have right now to preach in the power of the Name of Jesus? Will you be courageous and pray for boldness or even more boldness? It is up to us, God's people, to share the Gospel. That is how the Father has chosen to see the Gospel go forth: by using believers. It's not always easy. You may get rejected, you may get mocked, and you may get ridiculed and slandered. Will you obey the Great Commission anyway? Are you willing to obey God's Word and go into all the world to share the Gospel?

## Be Filled With the Spirit

We cannot walk by faith in boldness without being filled with the Spirit. We will only be filled with the Spirit when we are prepared to yield ourselves to the Lord Jesus Christ. Are you willing to yield to the Lord; to forsake and sacrifice everything for Him? If yes, then you are in for the ride of your life!!! If not, then you will NOT see the power of the Holy Spirit fully realised in your life. We see from the book of Acts that the filling of the Holy Spirit came through prayer *(Acts 13:2-3)*. We need to pray and ask God for the Holy Spirit to fill us. Evidence of the Holy Spirit filling us will be that we walk in power and that we will speak with boldness about Jesus. Why is there a lack of the workings of the Holy Spirit in power in the western church?

Maybe you could ask yourself the following questions. Are you surrendered to Jesus?

Are you leading a crucified life (that is obedience to God)? Are you praying daily?

The journey begins in the prayer closet. As you seek the Lord, He will be found by you. The presence of the Holy Spirit will lead you to live in the power of God if you are willing to pay the price of obedience. What is the price for walking in the power of God with all boldness? Obedience; absolute surrender. Will you do whatever the Spirit leads you to do and go wherever He leads you to go?

How do you learn obedience? By imitating Jesus. As you spend time in the Lord's presence and His Word, you learn obedience from Jesus who walked fully in God's way. But ultimately it's a choice. Will you choose to obey God? Peter and John had been with Jesus and they were filled with the Holy Spirit. They counted the cost and obeyed God rather than man, and many were saved, healed and set free because of their obedience.

Why has the Holy Spirit been given to us? One reason is so that we can preach the Gospel in boldness with signs and wonders following so we can display the power of God. But when we are seeing God move mightily, opposition steps up. You've only got to read the book of Acts to see that. Why does this happen? Satan does not want to see God's Kingdom come. As Christians, we have an enemy who hates us. This opposition may include threats, slander, lies, back-stabbing or something else. Are you willing to endure that for the sake of the Gospel? We need to lose sight of self and only see God. Are you ready for that? If not, get ready. Do not be afraid. Keep your eyes firmly fixed on Jesus at all times. It really does not matter what man thinks. The most important thing is what God thinks. May your deepest desire be to please the Lord and do His will.

Be willing.

Be available.

Be bold.

Be ready to preach the Gospel.

## Story of Jayden

The first time I met Jayden and his 15 year old friends was on a bitterly cold winter's night of 4°C when a few of us had gathered in the Mall to pray before going out 'fishing' for men. As we finished praying a group of four guys gathered near us and I knew God had brought them there for us to share the Gospel. They were quite mocking at first and very distracted, riding their skateboards around but I persevered as one of them was really paying attention. As I finished sharing with them a couple of teenage girls walked by on the other side of the Mall. Jayden called out to them to come over and hear about Jesus. They came over. This time I used my EvangeCube and that piqued the guys' attention too, so they listened in as well. They heard the Gospel twice that night! I gave them all Love Hobart cards which have my phone number on. Some of the guys started prank-calling me one after the other!

I met these guys again in McDonald's a few days later and they asked heaps of questions. The following Saturday Jayden text me to see if I was coming to do my 'street thing'. I said I'd be in at 7pm. At 6:30pm I got a phone call to ask where I was. I told them I'm on my way and I'll be there soon. There were about half a dozen of them when I arrived. As I started sharing the Gospel, they called others over and in the end there was a group of twelve of us in the Mall with me preaching! Then some of the guys wanted to do street evangelism with me.

Jayden is a born evangelist, he just doesn't happen to be saved yet. He was bold and courageous and willing to talk to anyone about Jesus. He said he'd like to be my assistant, and I said you'll need Jesus. I've seen him a few times since then, so I've shared the Gospel a lot with him. We continue to wait and pray for a move of God's Spirit amongst these young people.

Christianity is not about getting people to just say a prayer because they are emotional, but it's about the Holy Spirit moving in their hearts. We have to be willing to wait for the Holy Spirit to do this work of transformation in someone's life and it will be worth the wait. God's Word will not return void.

## Story of Travis

I first got to know Travis when we started Youth nights in 2015. He was always drunk! He would often come with alcohol in a soft drink bottle until we worked out what was going on. He would be quite verbally aggressive when drunk and was definitely lacking patience.

Week after week he would come to Youth and it was often quite hard work with Travis and his friends as there were nearly always fights. But over time we have seen a big change. Where Travis was once wagging school, always drinking and often in trouble with the Police, there is now a big turning around. Last year he started studying at TAFE with one of his friends. His friend bailed out just before completing their Cert 1 but Travis went onto do Cert 2 and now he's nearly finished Cert 3. We are very encouraged by the good change in Travis. He still comes to Youth and if we don't have many kids come, he'll tell me not to worry, that he'll bring everyone next week. Sure enough, he does. Occasionally Travis, who's from a Christian family, will come to church. Even though he's not walking with Jesus yet we trust one day soon he will be.

## The 3 M's

Evangelists train and equip the saints for the work of the ministry, and having come to the realisation that God has called me and gifted me as an evangelist, it is my awesome privilege to train and equip others in the body of Christ in being able to preach the Gospel.

One night in March 2015 I started getting inspiration for an evangelism seminar. Over the course of 2 hours I wrote down the outline and much of the content for a seminar, "Fearless Evangelism: How to share the Gospel in everyday life." Much of this will be shared in the following three chapters of this book. Although some tried to discourage me from running a seminar, saying I should only do training on the streets, my family and our team at Love Hobart were fully supportive. That April we ran our first Fearless Evangelism seminar with about 30 people in attendance and since then we've run it on numerous occasions, even in WA. My family take part in the seminar if they are available, as the ministry I do is mostly with my family. We've had lots of good feedback from the seminar, especially that it's practical and Biblical and a good starting point for those who know they should share the Gospel but don't know where to start.

The next three chapters in this book cover the three main points of the seminar which are:

1.  **Motive**- which needs to come from obedience to the Great Commission.
2.  **Message**- which is the truth: The Gospel. How to share the Gospel?
3.  **Manner**- which is love: having the compassion of Christ, and showing the Father's heart to people.

*"How then shall they call on Him in whom they have not believed? And how shall they believe in Him of whom they have not heard? And how shall they hear without a preacher? And how shall they preach unless they are sent? As it is written: 'How beautiful are the feet of those who preach the Gospel of peace, who bring glad tidings of good things.'"*

*Romans 10:14-15*

*"Radical obedience to Christ is not easy... It's not comfort, not health, not wealth, and not prosperity in this world. Radical obedience to Christ risks losing all these things. But in the end, such risk finds its reward in Christ. And he is more than enough for us."*

*David Platt*

## Chapter 3

# Motive

## Obedience to the Great Commission

How will the lost hear the Gospel? Through us!

God didn't choose angels to share the Gospel. He has chosen us, His people, to preach the Gospel. It's part of our calling. That is, ALL who are Christians. That doesn't mean you just do all you can to get the lost to your church so they can hear a sermon from your pastor. No. We all need to be ready to preach the Gospel in season and out of season, wherever we are. Unless the lost hear they can't repent, believe and be saved. And today, in Hobart at least, not many non-Christians are just walking into church to check out what Christianity is all about. More than ever, we need to get hold of the vision of the Great Commission to 'GO'. We will not all be evangelists but we're all called to preach the Gospel, wherever we go.

*"Go into all the world and preach the Gospel." Mark 16:15.*

Literally 'go' means 'in your going'. That is, in your going to work, to school, to the park, to the shops, to the gym, to the beach etc. That is, as you do life, be ready and available to share your faith. It won't always be convenient but will you be available for the Lord anyway? The Great

Commission is about obedience. Therefore the first step in preaching the Gospel is being willing to obey the Great Commission and not thinking you can leave it to everyone else. Are you willing? I like to call it Radical Obedience.

In Acts we read of the early church that was established by the power of God. Ananias and Sapphira had dropped dead because they lied, great fear had come on all the people, new believers kept being added to the church, and more healings and miracles happened (*Acts 5:14-15*). Were the apostles then loved and accepted by all the religious leaders because of all the good works they were doing amongst the people? No, that didn't happen. Now they were to face more opposition.

They got arrested; AGAIN *(Acts 5:17-18)!* Why? The leaders were annoyed and quite possibly jealous that the apostles were having a big impact on the people. The council was full of educated men who had no ministry of power, only tradition and religion. They were trying desperately to protect themselves and their dead traditions. The apostles on the other hand were ordinary lay people, but God was working powerfully through them. They had no thought for themselves but only that the Word of God be preached, and the signs and wonders, healing and miracles followed the preaching. So the authorities locked up the apostles! Quite possibly all twelve.

Remember they had not committed a crime. This unjust act was used as a means to try to silence the apostles, and to get them away from the people in the hope that there would be no more converts to Christianity. It was meant to bring shame on them and there by discredit them from God's work.

Isn't Satan still trying the same today? He is still trying to discredit true men and women of God through shame and slander, through false accusation and fabricated evidence. But those who truly belong to God will not be stopped from doing God's work in obedience. They will continue preaching the Gospel no matter what Satan tries throwing at them.

The apostles got locked up many times and God did not always intervene supernaturally but this time He did move supernaturally. An angel appeared in the prison and commanded the apostles to go and stand in the temple and preach Jesus. They weren't to hide or have secret meetings.

They weren't to save their lives by escaping to another city. They were to stay right there in Jerusalem, out in the open, in the public eye for all to see and hear the message of the Gospel. They were to continue in obedience and boldness.

These instructions were the exact opposite to what the religious leaders had said for the apostles to do. So who did they obey? There was immediate obedience to what the angel told them to do. As soon as the gates to the temple were opened they were there preaching. There was no putting off what they were told to do. There was no concern for themselves or the consequences of their obedience: just instant obedience to the Lord. If they had chosen to be silent instead, the rivers of living water that were flowing out of them could quite possibly have dried up and this new work would have come to nothing.

In the meantime the high priest and council sent to the prison for the apostles. But the officers checked the prison and found it empty even though it was still under guard. There was no evidence of locks being tampered with. There was no sign or evidence that anyone, let alone twelve apostles, had escaped! They wondered what had happened but they had no idea. This was an unbelievable situation but it was absolutely true. They could not explain what had happened. Then a report came in that the apostles were teaching in the temple again! Talk about persistence and obedience! But also think how strange this would have appeared as generally prisoners that managed to escape from prison would escape and hide for fear of being locked up again. But not these men. They were on their Father's business with renewed vigour to preach the Gospel to the people. This was RADICAL OBEDIENCE!

So again the apostles were arrested. Why did the angel let them out at night if they were still going to end up on trial? Maybe it was a testing of their willingness to obey God, but also in that extra time that they preached that morning there would have quite possibly been those who were hearing the words of life for the first time.

So the apostles were brought before the council again, but without force, for the authorities feared the people (although they didn't fear God). This was a full council which Satan meant to use to bring shame on the apostles, but God meant it for good. Those council members all got to hear the good news of the Gospel, where otherwise they may not have heard. The apostles were accused of disobeying the commands of authority. The council could have listened to the teachings of the apostles and been convicted but they ignored all of it. Pride stopped them receiving the truth. The council took offence that the apostles would put Jesus' blood on their hands. The response of the apostles was, 'WE OUGHT TO OBEY GOD RATHER THAN MAN'. There was no pride or self-will in this answer, but rather faithfulness to God. No matter their circumstances they would not compromise or keep quiet about Jesus no matter what any authority said to them.

God had commanded them to teach in the name of Jesus and they would not disobey God's command. And neither should we. They did not make excuses or beg for pardon but instead repeated the charge that Jesus' blood was on the council's hands. They pointed out the sin of the council again, laying the responsibility of Jesus' death on them. The apostles spoke of God's divine intervention; that although the council had tried disgracing Jesus, God raised and exalted Him by His power.

## The Outcome

The council was furious, but the apostles were perfectly composed. The truth made the council members angry, so they made plans to kill the apostles. But Gamaliel, a Pharisee, who was a highly esteemed scholar gave an alternative solution: wait and see. Time would tell. This was not the first time there had been a situation like this. Gamaliel said if the apostles are not of God they won't succeed but if they are of God nothing will stop this and the leaders may be coming against God Himself. They agreed with Gamaliel and so refrained from killing the apostles at this time. But they didn't want to just let them go. They wanted some kind of revenge against the apostles, so the apostles were all beaten. They endured physical pain through the beating. It was a brutal punishment which was unfair and unjust. This was done to shame them and also in the hope it would silence them. Again they were commanded not to speak. As the apostles yielded to God's will and suffered for Jesus they grew in obedience. They learned obedience through suffering. So they left and rejoiced. No complaining to God about why He'd let them be arrested and beaten, but rejoicing that they were counted worthy to suffer for Jesus. They bore their sufferings with cheerfulness as Jesus said to do.

*"Blessed are those who are persecuted for righteousness sake, for theirs is the kingdom of Heaven. Blessed are you when they revile and persecute you, and say all kinds of evil against you falsely for My sake. 'Rejoice, and be exceedingly glad, for great is your reward in Heaven, for so they persecuted the prophets who were before you.'" Matthew 5:10-12*

So did the apostles stop preaching? No, they kept doing what God had called them to do. They trusted God with the consequences of their actions, as they were determined to obey God and keep preaching the Gospel. So they continued daily in the temple and homes preaching Jesus as the Christ. That is, every day of the week. They would not stop preaching Jesus Christ: Christ and Him crucified. Christ and Him glorified. They continued in boldness and disregarded the threats of the council which, if they had obeyed, would have caused them to be disobedient to God.

For those who are being opposed in God's work, take comfort that those who oppose you are actually fighting against God. The insults, slander, backstabbing and even fabricated evidence that come against you are actually coming against God. If you suffer for preaching the Gospel, you too need to rejoice and be glad. Follow the example of Jesus and these apostles. You may face a different cost for your obedience today than what the apostles and the early church faced, but there is always a cost. Your one step of obedience could have an impact on many others. Are you obeying the Lord today? Don't be afraid, the Lord is with you. The cost of obedience can be great at times, but the blessing of obedience is greater. WE ALL NEED TO BE OBEDIENT TO THE GREAT COMMISSION. Will you speak boldly about Jesus no matter the cost? Are you fearful? Pray for boldness. Are you lacking courage? Pray for boldness. You don't know how to share the Gospel? Then learn.

## Are You Willing?

You may not know what God has in store for you. You may not know His plans for you but will you fully trust Him and His promises? Obedience to walk in God's ways when you say "Here I am Lord, use me" will see great victories come to pass that you could not have even thought possible. Do you know Him well enough so you can trust Him and say Lord I will do anything you're calling me to do?

## The Example of Philip and the Ethiopian Eunuch

In *Acts 8:26* we read of the angel of the Lord speaking to Philip telling him to leave Samaria and go to the desert road that led to Gaza. There was a revival happening in Samaria and Philip had been a big part of that, and now he was being asked to leave the place where all the action was (i.e. healings, miracles and many being delivered) to go to the desert. Philip's immediate response was obedience. Would you have obeyed immediately? How many times does the Lord ask you to do something and you don't obey? But if you don't obey how can God use you to do His will?

Unknown to Philip, there was an Ethiopian travelling in his chariot on this desert road. This wasn't just some ordinary Ethiopian but one of great authority *(Acts 8:29)*. The Holy Spirit directed Philip to go near and overtake the chariot. Again Philip obeyed. He was then directed by the Spirit to approach the Eunuch so he could step forward in confidence. This Ethiopian was reading Isaiah and couldn't understand it. He invited Philip into the chariot and he was then able to explain Isaiah to the Eunuch, preaching Jesus to him, which led to his salvation.

As we are led by the Spirit to go talk to people we need to obey God and be ready to explain the good news of the Gospel. As we walk in willing obedience to God He may well take us before people of influence. We must not be afraid to preach Jesus to the people that the Holy Spirit leads us to.

## What Can You Expect When You Obey God?

Opposition! Satan hates people obeying God. Whenever you do things for God you will be met with opposition by Satan. He is our adversary who opposes God and God's people and God's work, just as he did with the apostles. But, like the apostles, rejoice when you're opposed, counting it all joy that you've been counted worthy to suffer for Jesus.

Will there be a cost in your obedience to preach the Gospel? Probably. Are you willing to count the cost, whatever that looks like? It's easier to do this when you keep eternity in view, for you will be positioned on that great and final day for the Lord to come to you and declare publicly "good and faithful servant." May Jesus be glorified through your obedience.

Will it be out of your comfort zone to obey the Great Commission? Very likely. I know it is for me. And that's not just going up to strangers with the intention of sharing the Gospel, but also being out in the cold weather all through winter is uncomfortable as I really feel the cold. But I must say, the Lord has kept me in good health even though I've spent many a cold day out on the streets of Hobart sharing the Gospel.

## Hindrances to Obeying the Great Commission

Three of the most common hindrances to Christians being obedient in sharing the Gospel are fear, a lack of training in how to share the Gospel and a lack of love for the lost. Let's look at these three hindrances.

### 1. Fear

Many Christians are afraid about what could happen if they start sharing the Gospel. So what's the worst that can happen in Australia? My experience is a bit of verbal abuse but even that is very rare. Having shared the Gospel thousands of times I've only had a couple of really difficult experiences and a few times where people have mocked. One time we shared with a middle aged lady and she thought it was hilarious that we were out sharing our faith. She had studied religions, and she thought Christianity was just no good. We didn't stay long but as we walked off we could hear her laughing and laughing at us. I just felt sorry for her really. Her arrogance and intellect had blinded her to the truth.

Don't give into fear. Fear will incapacitate you. Get into the Word of God so your faith, as small as it might seem, can grow. Then see what God will do through you when you step out in obedience. Be ready, willing and prepared to GO, for God will not ask of you anything that you cannot do without His help.

He will give you all you need to do His will.

There can also be fear of man. What will people think of me? What will my friends think when they find out? To this I say: don't worry what people think, but be concerned about what God thinks.

*"The fear of man brings a snare, but whoever trusts in the LORD shall be safe." Proverbs 29:25*

Our fear of God needs to be greater than our fear of man. God is with us wherever we go and as we are on His business sharing the Gospel you can be sure the Lord is with you no matter what happens, and no matter where He leads.

## 2. Lack of Training

Many have not shared the Gospel because they haven't been trained how. That's one of the main reasons why I've written this book; to encourage and equip others to be obedient to the Great Commission. As you read through the next chapter you will be shown ways in which you can share the Gospel

### 3. Lack of love for the Lost

Daily we need to think about eternity, and remember that everyone that does not hear about Jesus will go to Hell forever. We are not here on this earth just to enjoy ourselves and pursue our own agenda but we are here to be available and to serve the Lord. Our minds need to be renewed and we may need to remind ourselves that there is an eternity looming and there are only two destinations—Heaven or Hell.

The Father loves the lost so much. We must remember we were lost once and through the preaching of the Gospel we have come to know Jesus as Lord and Saviour. The Father's heart is that none should perish but that all should come to Him (*John 3:17*). If you do not have a love for the lost you do not really know the Father's heart. For in knowing Him and His love we should be reflecting His love and the compassion of Christ to the lost. If you do not love the lost, get on your knees and cry out to God to give you that love. Without this love how can you bring Christ to this lost generation? And as Charles Spurgeon said, "Have you no wish for others to be saved? Then you're not saved yourself, be sure of that!"

## Check for Wrong Motives

Also check for wrong motives of looking good to man or trying to get your statistics up on how many people you've led to the Lord. It's so easy to have good intentions at the start and then fall into wrong motives. We have an enemy Satan who seeks to trip us up. Pride can creep in almost unawares if you're not checking your heart regularly (*Psalm 139:23-24*). Our motive needs to be obedience to our Lord and Saviour Jesus Christ, from a pure heart.

## A Prophecy Given to Me in 2012

"As you keep giving the bread I see a whole flock of birds coming to receive it. There's lots of birds; there's so many. They keep coming; they fill the sky. As you sow seed it will be received. They'll come."

## How Much Seed Are You Sowing?

So many people are praying for the harvest to come in; praying for revival; but they're not sowing seeds. In *2 Corinthians 9:6-7* it says what we sow we will reap. What seed are you sowing? A pumpkin seed will produce a pumpkin. You only get what you sow. If you're sowing the Gospel you'll reap converts. If you're sowing prayers of healing you'll reap healings. If you're sowing the Word of God you'll reap Disciples. If you're not sowing anything you won't reap anything.

He who sows sparingly will reap sparingly, whereas he who sows abundantly will reap abundantly. We also need to pray over our seeds that have been sown in faith that they will fall on good fertile ground that will bring forth a harvest of 30, 60 or 100 fold. Take responsibility to pray over your seed. No one else is necessarily going to do that for you. It is an effort to sow seed as it is for a farmer, but the harvest will be well worth it.

As you pray over your seeds and wait patiently for them to grow, the harvest will surely come, as God's Word will not return to Him void (*Isaiah 55:11*).

## Story of Matt

One night as I was walking back to the Mall with two of my daughters, I saw a group of kids on top of the toilet block near the park. We walked past them and even though there was about seven of them and it was dark I sensed it was right to stop and talk with them. They were all youth from various countries in Africa, and were happy enough to talk. One of them, Matt, was very against Christianity even though he'd been brought up in a Christian home. He didn't want to hear the Gospel or look at the EvangeCube, but the others did.

Over the next few weeks I bumped into this group of teens on a number of occasions in different locations around town.

Sometimes there'd only be a couple of them and other times there were other friends there. What was interesting was that if Matt was in that group he would tell the others, "You need to listen to her, she's going to tell you about Jesus." He would then say to me, "Tell them about Jesus they really need to hear." So Matt would open up the way for me to share the Gospel with his friends.

One day I was walking through the Mall and I saw Matt with a large group of his friends; some I knew and some I didn't. I called out to him, "Hi, how're you going Matt?" He replied, "Yeah, I'm good." I started to walk over to talk more. Then suddenly Matt put his hands over his ears and exclaimed in jest, "Oh no, I shouldn't have said 'Hello' to her, now she's going to come over and talk to me!" Not to be put off that easily, I did talk to him and his friends.

Many times when I saw Matt he was drunk or high on weed. I'd talk to him about the dangers of drunkenness and taking drugs but he continued to do those things. When we started Youth, Matt would often come along for a while but many times he and his friends were drunk or high. It was full-on and often chaotic, even crazy at times, but amidst it all, God was there.

One night at Youth, Matt was playing table tennis with his friend. After their game they had a play tousle and Matt fell into the wall (cement sheet) and put a hole in it! He was on the floor in agony in his tail bone. I quickly went over to him and offered to get an ambulance. But he was very insistent he did not want an ambulance. A few of my team members have first aid certificates so a few things were suggested but he said no to everything. I asked him if he would let me pray. He agreed to that. So kneeling down beside him on the floor I prayed. He stayed on the floor for a while, then slowly got up. He's a tough cookie, so wouldn't really let on how much pain he was in. He stayed for a while and then left. We kept asking if he was ok.

Later he told us that about 15 minutes after he left Youth that night the pain totally left and he never had any more trouble.

On the night my phone got stolen at Youth, Matt was one of the first who wanted to come to my aid and sort out the thief when found. (There are rumours as to who stole my phone but no actual evidence. I hope one day the thief will own up.)

Another time as I walked out of a shop, there was Matt and two of his friends I knew from street ministry coming up the street. They all gave me hugs and then Matt told me he had to go to court in the afternoon. I offered to go with him but he said there was no need. It was at 2:15pm and I had an appointment at 2pm so I couldn't go anyway. At 1:45pm my appointment got cancelled so I decided to go to court and find Matt. I couldn't see him anywhere but a security guard kindly showed me where he was. Matt was happy to have me come. His two friends were there too. We were sat in the crowded waiting room but I suggested we pray quietly. Well one of them decided we should all hold hands so the four of us held hands while I prayed. Shortly after, Matt, who was 17 years old at the time, was called into the juvenile court. In walked the four of us. Matt had to stand up the front near the judge and the rest of us sat at the back of the room. The judge asked if we were all family. This was quite funny to me as I have light skin and red hair and Matt and his friends are all dark-skinned with black hair. Matt turned and looked at the three of us and then turned to face the judge and replied with a hearty, 'Yes'. The judge looked at me and smiled as

I'm obviously not African but she carried on the proceedings as if that was normal. (I've had a good chuckle about this since). Matt had a very good outcome from court and so I took him and his two friends to a coffee shop for hot chocolates and 'God-talk', lots of it. They had heaps of questions. After 2 hours with them I again suggested we pray and thank the Lord for the good outcome for Matt. I said I could just pray with my eyes open so no one would know we were praying. But to this they replied, "We don't care what people think." They then put their hands together and bowed their heads. It was a long prayer as I prayed for each of them individually. The presence of God was so tangibly strong that when I said, 'Amen', they went, "Wow that was like having a high!" To this I replied, "Who needs drugs when you can have Jesus?"

Later Matt got his own place. I gave him one of my paintings. He was so excited to have this painting, he hugged it! He came to church for the first time shortly after. There were two girls outside on the grass so he invited them to church. He'd never met them before. He told them I had 10 kids. I reminded him I had 9. He said, "No you've got me as well so that's 10!" Then during our time of sharing testimonies in church, Matt got courage to share too. He started off by saying how he didn't like me the first few times I met him. He said how mean he was to me but I kept showing even more love the more he was mean which baffled him as he wasn't used to that. He then said he loved me and the other Africans did too, deep down in their cold hearts! He went onto say that we were making a difference out on the streets and not to stop because there are many kids out there that need us. What a blessing that was to us all to hear his words.

## Story of Toby

We first met Toby when we were running our free sausage sizzle in the park in October 2015. Although not tall in stature, Toby arrived with his big personality and skateboard. We warmed to him immediately and it wasn't long before he met all our family.

Toby has been through a lot of hard things in life including being alone in this world. It wasn't long before he started calling me Mum. That is a privileged position he's given me in his life.

Now the road has not been all easy in our contact with Toby. We've had a few run ins at times where he didn't like what we said and he would storm out of Youth banging the glass door as he went. But a week or two later he would show up again and sometimes there was a 'sorry Mum'.

Toby had a Christian upbringing but there is a lot of hurt there and it's hard for him to see where God is in all that he has walked through. We've had many a chat about God, His love for mankind, the hardships of life and more. Toby is still on a journey of finding the truth. We continue to love him and pray for him and invite him along to family activities as well as church and Youth while we continue to pray for him.

*"For so the Lord has commanded us: 'I have set you as a light to the Gentiles, that you should be for salvation to the ends of the earth' "*

*Acts 3:47*

*'Away with your milk and water preaching of the love of Christ which has no holiness or moral discrimination in it, away with the preaching of Christ that neglects that He was crucified for sin.'*

*Charles Finney*

## Chapter 4

# Message

## The Truth of the Gospel of Jesus

The Gospel is not necessary an easy message to give, but it is the truth. Don't water it down or be afraid of challenging people in love, as it is the truth that will set people free.

I've mentioned the EvangeCube a few times so I'm going to go through how I use it in my own words. The EvangeCube can be purchased from www.e3resources.com

Even if you don't have an EvangeCube you can still use the principles in the cube for sharing the Gospel.

## Using the EvangeCube to Share the Gospel

(Pictures used with permission e3Resources ©2017)

### Picture 1

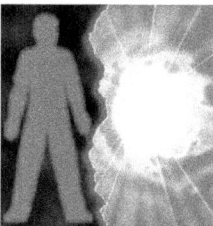

Do you know what sin is? We tend to think of sin as big things like murder, rape, violence, terrorism and the like. Then maybe other sins like lying, stealing, drunkenness and sexual immorality. But there can also be sins in the heart such as anger, hatred, greed, lust, jealousy, unforgiveness and selfishness. I then ask questions to find out where people are at. Do they think they have ever done any sin? Big or little? Anything at all? Most people admit they have, but for those who are a bit hesitant I ask them if they have loved the Lord God with all their heart, soul, mind and strength? If they haven't, that is a sin too.

I may ask if you were to measure your sin, on a scale of 1-100, 100 being perfect, where do you think you might be on that scale? I explain that to go to Heaven you need to be perfect, so if you have done any sin you cannot go to Heaven. Even if you think you're better than others that's not good enough. All of our sin separates us from God. God is perfect, pure and holy and we cannot come into His presence with our sin and we can't go to Heaven. Our sin is like black filth that we carry around. We can't see it, but God sees it.

Even though we have all sinned God loves us so much that He did something for us so that we can come into His presence and go to Heaven when we die. Do you have any idea what that could be?

## Picture 2

Jesus Christ the Son of God came to earth, born as a baby and grew up to become a man. The Bible says He was tested like us but He never sinned. So when He went to the cross, He was falsely accused as He hadn't actually done anything wrong. But it was all part of God's perfect plan of redemption, that Jesus became a sacrifice for us. He became a substitute as He died in our place. We couldn't do anything about our sin but Jesus Christ the Son of God became the perfect sacrifice for us. This is God's love in action that before we knew Him He loved us.

## Picture 3

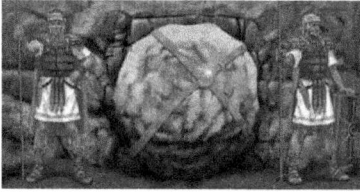

When Jesus died, His body was put in a tomb. There were guards assigned to the tomb as the authorities were concerned that Jesus' disciples would try stealing His body and pretend He had risen from the dead.

## Picture 4

On the third day Jesus rose again. He is a living Saviour. He's not dead He's alive! He paid the price for our sin.

## Picture 5

There is only one way to heaven, and that is through Jesus. He died for our sin. Buddha didn't die for sin, Muhammad didn't die for sin; they couldn't, they were not perfect. No other religion deals with the consequences of sin, in fact they're all just trying to be good enough to get to Heaven or be reincarnated, depending on their belief.

Nobody can be good enough to go to Heaven, no matter how good they try to be, because sin stops us- all sin; big and small. That is why God the Father sent His Son Jesus to die for us, so that all who call on His name will be saved. This is perfect love.

## Picture 6

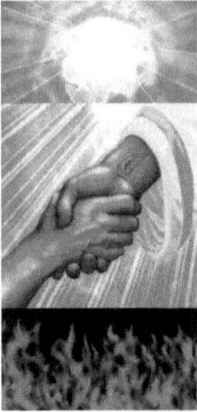

To become a Christian you need to repent of your sin and ask Jesus to be your Saviour and Lord. In accepting Jesus as Saviour, you need to confess your sin and repent of your sin with the intention that you flee from sin. In accepting Jesus as Lord you give up the right to live for yourself and now choose to live for God first. He is a jealous God and He requires first place in your life. There is no room for Him to be second, fifth or any other place; only first. There is a cost in being a Christian, you must lay your life down, but I can testify God is faithful.

So, if what I've said is the truth and you were to die in the next 20 seconds, where would you go: Heaven or Hell? If they think they would go to Heaven because they haven't done anything really bad you need to explain again the need to be perfect not just 'good'. Explain that ALL sin separates us from God whether we think it's big or small. Many think it's only criminals that go to Hell, so we need to be willing to patiently explain again that we have all fallen short of God's standard of perfection.

## Picture 7.

As a Christian we need to pray, read the Bible daily and meet with other Christians to grow, be encouraged and discipled.

Then even young Christians need to be encouraged to share the Gospel. We do all this as an outworking of God's love.

When I've finishing sharing the Gospel and answering questions I ask if they would like a Bible. I give out good quality, brand new pocket Bibles with large print in a variety of colours as I believe this is the most important book they can ever read. Sometimes people will say 'no' to a Bible initially but when I show them the Bibles they often change their minds. I also offer a tract. I use 'Why Jesus?' by Alpha. Then I ask if I can pray for them; a 30 second prayer, no longer. I ask if there's anything specific they would like prayer for. If not, I just pray a blessing on them. It can be helpful for people to hear how you pray as they may not have heard anyone pray before. I also tell them I'll pray with my eyes open so that anyone passing by won't know we're praying as I'm not there to embarrass anyone.

## My Young Friends Who Use the EvangeCube

A few years ago, if someone had told me that I'd be doing all that I am now, I would have thought they were making it up. My life is surely nothing like I could have imagined. Then on top of that there are things that happen on the streets that just blow me away. One of the most amazing things for me has been to see the eagerness of some of these young people to use my EvangeCube and share it with others. And these kids aren't saved yet! It's like discipleship back to front, but that's how things have panned out for us.

## Story of Rocky

I remember the first time I met Rocky was the third night I had started meeting kids on a Friday at Subway for food and God-talk. He was one of the twenty or so that showed up that night. I didn't see him again for a while but whenever I did he was always very polite and helpful. As I got to know Rocky more, he would bring friends for me to meet so I could share the EvangeCube with them. One night at Youth, Rocky called himself my apprentice. From there I thought if he's going to be my apprentice that he should have his own EvangeCube. I gave him a cube much to his delight, and he also took a handful of my ministry cards I give out on the streets. He'd periodically ask for more cards as he ran out.

On the day that I was verbally abused in the alley (see Chapter 2), Rocky was the one that told the lady that was lying about me to leave. Later when I thanked him for doing that he said, "Anytime, Helen. Always have your back."

Rocky has been to our home quite a few times, and to church on a number of occasions too. Our family has all got to know him well. He has enjoyed hanging out with us and seeing what Christian's do for fun. It's been great getting to know him.

Although he's moved away from Hobart at the moment, we keep in touch, and we continue to pray for him.

## Story of Oscar

In October 2016 I walked up to the alley and saw Oscar there with a couple of other guys. We chatted for a while and it was getting close to lunch time so I offered to take them to Subway to get a 'foot long'. They were a bit hesitant to start with, not wanting me to 'waste' my money. But I explained I was happy to shout them as long as we had some more 'God-talk'. They were so appreciative, so off we trotted to Subway. As we ate lunch one guy had to leave but Oscar and the other guy spent over an hour with me. I answered their many questions and explained the Gospel using the EvangeCube.

Later that afternoon I was in the Mall talking to a young mum I've got to know, Hayley, and a friend of hers. As we were talking, along came Oscar and his friend. They knew the young mum as well, so came over to say, "Hello". Oscar decided to tell Hayley's friend about Jesus using my EvangeCube. He did an excellent job considering he'd only heard it once. Then Oscar said, "Let's pray and hold hands". I asked him if he'd like to pray. He said he would. He asked, "Do you just start with, 'Dear Lord?'" I said that would be fine and to be respectful in his prayer. We all held hands and he prayed. Then when he'd finished he asked everyone to think of one thing they could give thanks for. Then we all said, "Amen". And all this was in the middle of the Mall outside Target!

A few weeks later I bought a pizza and went to the park to see who I could find who was hungry. There was Oscar and a couple of his friends who hadn't seen the EvangeCube before. Oscar asked if he could show them my cube and again he went through it and did an excellent job. There are some really awesome kids around Hobart and this was so encouraging for me to see.

## Graham

One day I was in a coffee shop with some kids and Graham asked if I had the 'box thing'? I wasn't sure what he meant to start with but then it clicked, he meant the EvangeCube. I pulled it out and asked him and the others to tell me what all the pictures meant. They did quite well, but it also showed me it's good to reinforce the message of the Gospel time and time again as it often doesn't sink in the first time it's heard.

## WARNING

Don't share a false message to entice people into saying a prayer or making a commitment if you haven't explained the Gospel. Telling someone that God will give them everything they want is not the truth. He's not a sugar-daddy God and we are commanded not to make a god in our own image. Neither should you tell someone to come to Jesus so their life will be easy. That's not true either, because as soon as you're saved you will have an enemy Satan who hates you and will come against you. The truth is:

> *"You therefore must endure hardship as a good soldier of Jesus Christ."* 2 Timothy 2:3

> *"Take up your cross daily and follow Jesus."* Luke 9:23

> *"Be sober, be vigilant, because your adversary the devil is as a roaring lion."* 1 Peter 5:8

## Preach the Truth

It's the truth that sets people free, and the truth is Jesus. Half- truths won't save anyone. If you really think there's no cost to being a Christian is it because you're not passionate for Jesus? Have you become lukewarm? Be a threat to Satan's camp. If you are a threat to the enemy's camp you will be in battles, that's a certainty. You've only got to read about the apostles to know that.

We are called to be mighty, on-fire, passionate, bold and courageous Christians. Be sure to preach the Gospel of the Bible: that is, the same Gospel that the apostles preached. Don't be afraid to talk about the cross, sin, consequences of sin, repentance, Heaven and Hell. Sometimes people will get annoyed but that's often because they're under conviction of sin. Unless they have humility, they will resist the Spirit of God.

> *"God resists the proud but gives grace to the humble."* 1 Peter 5:5b

## Salvation

Generally, people need a conviction of sin to precede coming to Christ. As Jesus said, 'Repent and believe'. Sin separates us from God. The cross is the only means to bring us back to God. If we bypass the need for repentance, we don't need the cross.

We need to explain the Gospel fully and not try to get a 'quick' salvation. There have been times when people I've shared the Gospel with didn't make a commitment immediately, but that night they went home and in the quiet of their bedroom accepted Jesus as Lord and Saviour.

## Using Questions to Share the Gospel

This way of sharing the Gospel was originally based on what I learnt from Ray Comfort's teaching in 'The Way of the Master'. It involves asking questions, but over the years I have modified what I ask to be more appropriate for our Australian culture and also the age of the people I generally share with. Some of the questions I use are as follows:

- Have you ever been to church?
- Did you get to go to Sunday school as a child?
- Have you had a Christian up-bringing?
- Have you ever thought about God?
- Have you thought about what will happen to you when you die?
- Do you know what the Father did so you can have eternal life so you don't go to Hell?
- Are you a good person?
- How good do you have to be to go to Heaven?
- Have you ever lied?

- Have you ever stolen anything, even something little?
- Have you ever taken the name of the Lord in vain?
- Have you ever lusted after a woman, that is, to commit adultery in your heart?
- When you stand before God on judgement day will you be innocent or guilty?
- If God were to judge you today by what you've done would you go to Heaven or Hell? If they say Hell, then ask does that concern you? If they say Heaven then ask how they think they're going to get into Heaven as they've admitted they've sinned against God.

Then give the message of hope that we have in the Gospel that Jesus died on the cross for our sins. He was buried and rose again the third day. Tell them they can come to Jesus today if they repent of their sins and ask Jesus to be Lord of their life.

## My 5-point summary for Sharing the Gospel

I have written out this 5-point summary, which you could memorise, or maybe write on a card and put it in your wallet for quick reference if you are likely to forget. As you're sharing the Gospel check you've covered these areas.

1. **Sin**- the problem, nobody is good enough to go to Heaven.
2. **The cross**- the remedy for sin; Jesus, the Way, the Truth and the Life. The Gospel.
3. **Repentance**- humility- confess your sins and turn away from them. Get right with God.
4. **Saviour**- Jesus- confess sins- receive Him by faith.
5. **Lord**- live for Jesus not self. He needs to be first.

*"Jesus said, 'The time is fulfilled, and the Kingdom of God is at hand. Repent and believe in the Gospel.'" Mark 1: 1*

For salvation to occur, generally speaking, one needs a conviction of sin to precede coming to Christ. As Jesus said, 'Repent and believe'. That is because sin separates us from God. The cross is the only means to bring us back to God. If we bypass the need for repentance we don't need the cross. The Gospel message includes the mention of sin separating us from God. We may need to explain what sin is, as it's not just big sin like murder, rape or terrorism. It's ALL sin. Even ungratefulness is a sin.

*"For He made Him who knew no sin to be sin for us, that we might become the righteousness of God in Him." 2 Corinthians 5:21.*

We need to present the true message of Jesus Christ and Him crucified, according to the Word of God. We need to make sure we are preaching the truth of Jesus, the Rock, and the Word. Then on that foundation we can build. If experience precedes the foundation of the Word, it can very easily lead to a need for 'feeling' God instead of being grounded in 'knowing Christ'. As you share the Gospel with the lost you need to speak of Christ and Him crucified so that the truth of your words, empowered by the Holy Spirit, can penetrate the hearts of the hearers. The Holy Spirit may well back your testimony up with healings, miracles, signs and wonders, but you need to be sure you lay the right foundation from the start. 'God loves you' is not the whole Gospel, but 'Christ died for you' will set us apart from the other religions as the power of the cross is the foundation of our faith. We must always remember the precious blood of Jesus that sets Christianity apart from any other religion and that Jesus is the only way to the Father.

People need to hear the message of the Gospel and understand what Jesus did for them. To truly understand the message of salvation they need to understand what Jesus came to save them from. Some people will have more understanding than others. Be willing to explain things simply but with the whole truth. We have all sinned (explain what sin is), and we've all fallen short of God's standard of perfection, but Father

God gave us His only Son Jesus as a substitute for our sin. Be patient and willing to repeat the Gospel again and again if the person you've shared with doesn't understand it.

If you wait for someone to ask you about God you could wait a very long time. Generally we'll need to be the ones to take the lead. Choose to direct the conversation into the things of God. A simple question or two can open up the way for you to share the most precious gift of all; the message of the Gospel. We have this rich treasure which is to be shared.

## Learn Some Key Verses

*"From that time Jesus began to preach and to say, "Repent, for the kingdom of Heaven is at hand." Matthew 4:17*

*"For God so loved the world that He gave His only begotten Son, that whoever believes in Him, should not perish but have everlasting life. For God did not send His Son into the world to condemn the world, but that the world through Him might be saved." John 3:16-17*

*"Nor is there salvation in any other, for there is no other name under Heaven given among men by which we must be saved." Acts 4:12*

*"For all have sinned and fallen short of the glory of God." Romans 3:23*

*"If you confess with your mouth The Lord Jesus and believe in your heart that God has raised Him from the dead, you will be saved." Romans 10:9*

*"... that Christ died for our sins according to the Scriptures, and that He was buried, and that He rose again the third day, according to the Scriptures ..." 1 Corinthians 15:3-4*

*"For by grace you have been saved through faith, and that not of yourselves; it is the gift of God, not of works, lest anyone should boast." Ephesians 2:8-9*

# How to Share the Gospel in 1 Minute

There will always be occasions where you have a very limited amount of time to share the Gospel with someone. Don't miss that opportunity by being unprepared. Rather have a practice at sharing the Gospel in 1 minute. Following are three different examples.

## Example 1

If you were to die tonight where would you go? There's two options; Heaven and Hell. To go to Heaven you need to be perfect, but you're not and neither am I. Any sin you or I have done stops us from entering Heaven. But God knew that we couldn't be good enough to go to Heaven so He made a way for us Himself. He sent His Son, His only Son, Jesus, to die on the cross in our place. He took the sin of the whole world.

God's desire is that none should perish. If you will repent and believe and accept Jesus as Lord and Saviour of your life you will be saved.

## Example 2

There is a God in Heaven who loves you with a passion. Do you know what God the Father did for you so that you could spend eternity with Him in Heaven? He sent His Son Jesus to earth.

Jesus lived a perfect life, never sinning or falling into temptation. He was falsely accused and ended up on a cross. But this was all part of God's plan to redeem (save) mankind, all because God loves us. The Bible says if you will repent and believe, that is to turn away from sin and accept Jesus as Saviour and Lord you will be saved. For Jesus did not come to condemn the world but to save the world.

## Example 3

Sin, all sin, separates us from God. We have all sinned and fallen short of God's standard of perfection. We are unable to go to Heaven in our own strength or because of our own goodness as we are not good enough! No, not one of us. We've all failed because of our sin. Amazingly God has still made a way for us to go to Heaven. He provided a substitute for us, someone else to bear the cost of our sin. This is why Jesus died on the cross for our sins. Now God says that if we repent and believe in the Lord Jesus Christ, then He will forgive our sins and give us eternal life with Him.

After a bit of practice, you'll find the Gospel quickly and easily rolls off your tongue. There are so many who have never heard this message. Even if you only have one minute that is enough time to sow a seed into someone's life that God can use.

## What's the Difference Between Christianity and All Other Religions?

When someone says they know about religions, that they've studied religions or they've studied Christianity, I find it helpful to ask these ones if they know what the difference between Christianity and all other religions is? Rarely do they know. The answer is that all other religions have no way of dealing with sin. They're trying to work their way to be good enough to go to Heaven or to be reincarnated depending on their religion.

None of us can be good enough to go to Heaven. Only Jesus could pay the price for sin, not Buddha or Muhammad or any other prophet as they were all sinful. Jesus Christ is the only One who has ever lived who committed no sin. As the perfect Son of God, He became a perfect sacrifice who was able to pay the price for our sins.

## Definitions

In sharing the Gospel in the West today it is good to be able to explain Biblical terms, words and phrases in everyday English to clarify what we are saying. Following are some of my explanations of Biblical words.

*Repentance-* literally means to have a change of mind. My simple definition is to confess your sins to God, asking Him to forgive your sins, with the intention that you want to stop sinning, and with God's help do a 180 degree turn away from your sin.

*Lord-* means to accept Jesus as first place in your life while no longer living for self.

*Sanctification-* is to be set apart for the Lord through the process of being cleansed from your sins as you turn your back on sin.

*Justification-* is the act of God whereby we are declared righteous by virtue of us being one with Christ. Simply put, it's 'just as if I'd never sinned.'

## Helpful Illustrations

Over the years I have read and heard of different illustrations which I've modified to suit my location and the people I meet.

### Elephant Illustration

I originally heard this from Vishal Mangalwadi but I have adjusted it for my audience. This illustration is particularly helpful when people say there's no way of knowing the truth.

There are five blind men and they're all given a different part of an elephant—one the leg, one the trunk, one the tail, one the ear and one the body. Each blind man is asked to describe what he thinks he is holding. The first one says a tree trunk,the second one says a hose, the third one says a rope etc.They all think the other is wrong, and it doesn't seem that the truth is knowable to these blind men. But along comes someone who can see, who tells them that they all have different parts of an elephant. This helps us to understand that we can know the truth from someone who reveals truth, who knows the bigger picture. In our case, God has revealed truth to us and so we can know the truth.

The following three illustrations I originally heard from 'Way of the Master' by Ray Comfort.

## Parachute Illustration

You're in an aeroplane and someone gives you a parachute as they know the plane is going to crash. But you don't put on the parachute because you don't believe them. Unless you put on the parachute it won't be of any help to you. Many people know about Jesus, but unless they put on the Lord Jesus, accepting Him as Lord and Saviour, He won't save them.

## Court Room Illustration

You've committed a crime. You're brought before a judge. The judge asks you, "Did you commit the crime?" You answer, "Yes", but you tell him you're a pretty good person really. You give money to charities, you do volunteer work, and you even go to church. But the judge is a just judge and because of that he needs to punish the crime that's on trial. You are ordered to pay a million dollars or go to jail for 12 months. You tell the judge you don't have a million dollars. So you are about to get taken off to jail but a man, who you don't know, walks through the courtroom door with a big bag in his hands. He stands before the judge and puts the bag on the desk in front of the judge and says, "I'm paying the fine for my friend. Here's a million dollars." The conditions have been met and you're let off. This illustration is a loose analogy for what God did for us in sending Jesus to die on the cross.

## Illustration to Use with Atheists

If I had a painting with me here, then we would know that there had been an artist who painted it, as the evidence is the painting. Then point to a building and ask if there was a designer (architect) that designed the building and engineers, builders, electricians etc. all involved in seeing the building come to existence? Now look at you and me. The evidence of a creator is the creation. And look how complex we are. We can say to that building, "Jump!", but it wouldn't jump in a million years. But if I say to you, "Jump!" you can say to me, "Take a hike", "Yes", "No" or "How high?" We have the ability to think and to make choices unlike anything made by man. We have been made by God, in the image of God.

# What Gospel are You Preaching?

Are you preaching the truth or falsehood? Following are some examples of false messages that I've heard.

1. 'Connect with God'. There's no mention of Jesus, sin or repentance. Buddhists and others will respond to this. This message is inoffensive to the masses but it is NOT the truth.

2. 'Say this prayer, you're a Christian now.' Again, there's no mention of the cross or repentance. No mention of sanctification or holiness, just words without the power of God to bring salvation.

3. 'Just lead a good life and you'll be fine!' This is what other religions teach. Just do more good than bad and you'll be Ok. But this is another false message.

*"For there is none righteous, no, not one." Romans 3:10*

*"for all have sinned and fall short of the glory of God." Romans 3:23*

## Different Outcomes from Paul's Preaching

In *Acts 17:5* we read of an uproar in Thessalonica after Paul preached because of envy from some of the Jews. Paul moved onto Berea, but the envious Jews from Thessalonica followed him and stirred up the crowds there too *(Acts17:13)*. Then Paul escaped to Athens where he preached the Gospel *(Acts 17: 32- 34)*. Some people mocked but there were some that believed. Later, in *Acts 18:6* we read about Paul in Corinth where he was opposed and the people blasphemed God, but many Corinthians also believed *(Acts 18:8)*. The Lord encouraged Paul to keep speaking out *(Acts 19: 8-10)*. Then in Ephesus there were riots from Paul's preaching followed by false accusations against Paul *(Acts 19:21-4.)* Preaching the Gospel is not always easy!

What Can You Expect When You Preach the Truth? You can expect Satan to stir things up for you and you will get different reactions from people: some good and some not so good. Some hear and receive the truth and some don't. Satan is not at all concerned about false, watered down messages of the Gospel being preached, the 'feel good' messages to tickle the ears of sinners. But he hates the true message that is the POWER of God to SALVATION. But know that God is FOR the one who speaks His Word BOLDLY and UNCOMPROMISINGLY.

We're here to serve the Lord and please Him, not man. Hatred, envy and jealousy from others will come. It will be no different to what Jesus and His disciples endured.

The New Testament church did not entice people to come to God through telling them what an amazing experience they had. Even on the day of Pentecost when they had just been baptized with the fire of the Holy Spirit, they kept the main thing, the main thing. They preached the Gospel of Jesus Christ. There is only one way to God and that is through Jesus. So preach the Gospel as it is the power of God to salvation. The Holy Spirit is the one who backs up the preaching of the Gospel. It's not about us trying to make something happen.

The devil is defeated through the preaching of the Word. That is why the devil has tried very hard to get Christians to either not preach the Word at all or if they are preaching, to entice Christians to share a fake, watered-down, 'feel-good' but powerless message.

## What is the True Message?

Christ crucified and resurrected for our sins. Repent and believe and be baptised. The outcome of this 'hard' message on the day of Pentecost? The people were cut to the heart, and 3,000 were saved that day *(Acts 2)*. There was no fluffy message, no compromise, no entertainment or performance, no mention of 'feel-good' experiences: just the preaching of the Word in truth. Oh, but some will say we can't talk to people in our society like that, they might get offended. Let them get offended! The true Gospel will bring offence but the Gospel message of the Bible is still the same and is still for today. If we try to water it down and make it more palatable to our generation we are in rebellion to God and we lose sight of the very power of our message. It's not a soft message people need or an entertaining church meeting but the truth. Only the truth will set them free. And the truth is Jesus. Proclaim the power of the cross and the Holy Spirit will back up the preaching of the Gospel. But He will not back up false messages.

## Outcome of False Preaching

As there has been a lot of false preaching in our generation there are many people who think they're saved but they're not. They do not live as one who walks with Jesus Christ as Lord and Saviour. There is no fruit.

They have never repented. They never counted the cost, and now their hearts and minds have become hardened to hear the truth. May it never be said of you or me that we preached a compromised message.

*"Let your gentleness be evident to all."*

*Philippians 4:5*

*"Young men and old men, and sisters of all ages, if you love the Lord, get a passion for souls. Do you not see them? They are going down to Hell by thousands; as often as the hand upon the dial completes its circuit, Hell devours multitudes, some of them ignorant of Christ, and others wilfully rejecting Him."*

*Charles Spurgeon*

# Chapter 5

# Manner

## The Love and Compassion of Christ

### How to Approach People

Approach others as you would like to be approached. That is, do to others what you would want them to do to you. Be courteous. Be respectful. Be gentle.

I usually introduce myself first. For example:

"Hi I'm Helen. I'm a pastor. Do you know what that is?" Mostly young people don't know what a pastor is so I explain I'm a Christian and I do a lot of street work in Hobart. That explains why I'm talking to them. I then ask if I can share the Gospel. I am a representative of Christ, so all that I do, I endeavour to show Christ's compassion, love and care.

Watch your tone of voice and body language. If you come across as judgemental you probably won't get a listening ear. But when God's love is flowing out of you, you will be like a bright light shining in the darkness.

*"Let all that you do be done in love." 1 Corinthians 16:14*

We need to love the people the Lord brings across our path, showing no partiality to the rich or the poor. Can we love people the way the Lord loves people? They may be dirty, smelly, homeless, hungry, hurting, broken, sick, deceitful, or angry but the Word of God says, "Love never fails". Let your genuine Christ-like love be evident to all. If you don't have this love, ask God to give it to you.

## How Can You Grow in Confidence to Approach People?

Learn how to be friendly. Practice does help. It's useful to get comfortable in approaching strangers. Start with just a smile or by saying, "Hi". Most people are usually happy enough to respond, it's only a small handful that aren't. Then ask how their day has been, or ask them about the weather or any small talk that comes to mind. Next, take a deep breath, pray quietly for courage, be bold and open your mouth and turn the conversation into the things of God.

## How to Start a Conversation about God

Following are some suggestions on how to turn a conversation into the things of God. The first two suggestions are particularly helpful with someone that you know well but you've been too scared to talk to about Jesus.

1. "I've just been to a training seminar to learn how to share what I believe as a Christian. Could I practise on you?" (I encourage people to use this after coming to my training seminar on Fearless Evangelism.)
2. "I've just been reading a book on evangelism and I was wondering if I could practise on you what I've learnt."

3.    Use third person. I often do this with older people. I explain what I do on the streets and then I share what I say with the young people. I would say something like this.

"This is how I share the Gospel with young people. I talk to them about what sin is and then I ask them if they think they've ever done any sin etc."

4.    "Do you know what Christianity is about? Would you please let me explain it to you?"

5.    "Have you ever been to church?"

6.    "Do you have any Christian friends?"

## Learn How to Break Into a Conversation

Remember, waiters break into conversations all the time, so don't be afraid to break into a conversation, politely of course. I often do this when there's a bigger group of people. Get bold, get courageous! Don't used puffed up titles about who you are, just say your name and what you do. Then be courageous to turn the conversation into the things of God.

## Ask Permission to Share

Where possible, I find it very helpful to ask permission to share my faith. This is being polite, respectful, courteous and compassionate, as above all we must have LOVE. When people are happy to hear, I often ask how long do I have? How long till your bus comes? Would you give me 1 minute, 2 minutes or 5 minutes?

## When People Say 'No'

If people say no, I don't push it, but often I can sense if there is still a bit of an openness. So sometimes I get in with a question.

For example, "Do you know what's the main difference between Christianity and all other religions?" or I'll say something like, "It's freezing cold (as it often is in Hobart) and I could be home in the warmth but I've chosen to be out here on the streets as I really believe this is the most important message you will ever hear. I can share it in one minute if you'll allow me?" Of course, I don't do this all the time as we need to be sensitive to the leading of the Holy Spirit but I have done this a lot. We are representatives of God and His love. Let all that you do be done in love. Even when people have said they don't want to hear about Christianity, some questions on more general things can build some rapport and then still open the way to share the Gospel.

Of those that say they are not interested in the Gospel I probably still get to share the Gospel with 80% of them. How do I do that? Each person is different and each situation is different but I have the Holy Spirit living in me and He is a good helper. Sometimes I'll just continue to talk about more general things and as the conversation progresses I'll start bringing in the things of God. I've had atheists and Muslims and others all say no initially to hearing the Gospel but following are a couple of stories of people I was still able to share with even though they initially said no. But at all times we need to remain gentle, compassionate and respectful as we represent Christ.

## Stories of People That Said 'No'

After sharing the Gospel with a couple of girls I saw a guy in his early twenties sitting forward on his seat in the park with his elbows on his knees and his hands on his chin with a hoody pulled over his head. I really had a very strong sensing I should go and talk to him. As soon as I said I was a pastor he told me he was an atheist and he wasn't interested in talking. I could tell he was very down and so, ever so gently, I asked him if he was Ok. Amazingly he started opening up and we ended up talking for about 45 minutes. I was able to share the Gospel in the end and he allowed me to pray for him too!

On another occasion, I was with my daughter Charity near the Bus Mall. We approached 2 guys, who, very soon into our conversation, told us they were Muslim. They were both from the Middle East, and were in Hobart finishing off their studies in engineering. As soon as they found out we were Christians they said they did not want to talk to us anymore. So we talked for an hour! How did that happen? It's hard to know exactly but I said something and they responded and I ended up hearing about Islam and they heard about Jesus.

Interestingly one of the guys had been reading the Bible and had a lot of questions about Christianity. My husband joined us towards the end, and being an engineer, he had a lot in common with them. At the end of our conversation they let me pray for them. The one who had been reading the Bible shook hands with us all, but the other one would only shake hands with David, as it was against his religion to shake hands with females. We blessed them and left.

Sometimes a 'no' isn't a no. But there's been other times where people have said no they don't want to hear and I just walk away. It really comes down to being sensitive to the leading of the Holy Spirit. The more I've done street ministry the easier it has become to sense the Spirit's leading.

## Appropriateness of Who to Talk To

In this day and age it pays to be very wise in who you talk to. For example if two burly, middle-aged Christian men were approaching teenage girls with the intention of sharing the Gospel, it could be very easily misconstrued as stalking, or sexual or something else. I would highly recommend that older Christian men DO NOT approach teenage girls to share the Gospel. Leave that to the women. There's plenty of guys out there that need to hear about Jesus. Obviously if you're sat on an aeroplane next to someone of the opposite sex if you're gentle and not pushy it may well be appropriate to share your faith. Be wise at all times.

## Stories from the Streets

One night David and Brodie got talking to a guy called Jason. He had had a Christian background but had been terribly hurt by a few different things including a broken marriage. Some months later my daughter and I approached a guy in Franklin Square to share the Gospel and unbeknown to us, it was Jason. He remembered David and Brodie and we had a good chat. A few weeks later I met him again and I remembered his name which was a big deal as I have so much trouble remembering names due to the sheer volume of people I talk to. He was impressed I'd remembered his name (and so was I!) which was definitely a God-thing. I asked if I could pray for him. He said because I'd remembered his name he'd let me pray next time. Well guess what? Within a week I bumped into him again, and yes, he let me pray for him. We are now friends on Facebook and he has said one day he's going to come to church. Still waiting for that, but at this time, it is often a slow process of reaching people for Jesus.

## Be Willing to Answer Questions on Anything

Give brief answers, which keep to the point. That is, cut out rambling. I've had people come out on the streets with me who just talk about all the intricate details of their lives when asked a simple question. For example, if someone is waiting for a bus there is often limited time to talk, so it is good to give brief answers. Examples of some of the questions I've been asked: Have you sinned? What's the biggest sin you've done? Did you have sex before marriage? Do you speed? Do you jay walk? What do you think about homosexuals? Have you ever done an exorcism? (I explain I call it deliverance and that Hollywood has exaggerated what really happens.) Interestingly this question comes up a lot.

Don't lie to cover up your sin, even past sin when asked about what you have done. Be real, don't be a hypocrite. Lying isn't the answer. Be honest. If you've led a life that you're ashamed of, talk about how God set you free from all of that; that you're now a new creation in Christ Jesus. We need to be living examples of Jesus Christ. That is, to be holy as He is holy.

*"But as He who called you is holy, you also be holy in all your conduct, because it is written, 'Be holy, for I am holy'." 1 Peter 1:15-16*

If you're talking about being holy but not living a holy life, it will nullify your testimony. Even something as simple as swearing; people know that Christians shouldn't do that. If you're living a hypocritical life as a Christian, the word of your testimony will not be powerful. Get right with the Lord and allow the Holy Spirit to bring correction.

## On-going Contact with People

Be willing to give your contact details so people can contact you. It can be important for people you share the Gospel with to have a way to contact you again if they desire, but without the pressure of them having to give you their details. Be careful not to ask for phone numbers of people especially if they're under age. Always exercise wisdom when asking strangers for their details, or when giving out yours as it could be an open door for trouble. Let the Holy Spirit guide you.

## Story

Sometimes I get a text message a year or two after meeting someone. It usually starts with, "You probably don't remember me but ..." Then they go onto tell me of something I said to them or did for them and now they want to catch up or have a text conversation. This happened recently with a girl I met 2 years ago. She said I'd stayed with her in the Bus Mall for her bus to come as she was alone and it was dark and there were a few 'strange' people around. I remembered that. She had just had a baby, 9 weeks premature, when she contacted me. I was then able to pray for her baby.

## Faithfully Sowing Seed

Be willing to sow the seed of the Gospel and let God work. That can be hard as you may never see that person again but are you sharing with them to make yourself feel good or because you genuinely desire them to know the truth and understand that you may just be one link in a chain? In eternity you will see the impact of your seed sowing. Don't try and push someone into saying a prayer of salvation, unless the Holy Spirit is truly moving. It's our job to preach the Gospel but it's the Holy Spirit that will bring people to the point of conviction and repentance. Let the Holy Spirit do His work. Pushing someone to say a prayer when they're not ready or because they're just feeling emotional usually backfires, and oftentimes their hearts become hardened as they feel tricked into being a 'Christian'.

## In Finishing off a Conversation, Offer to Pray

After I've shared the Gospel, answered questions and offered a Bible and/or a tract, when appropriate, I will ask if there is anything I could pray for them. I explain I'll pray with my eyes open so that if anyone is walking past they won't know I'm praying. I also tell them the prayer will be 30 seconds or less. I have had many, many people let me pray for them. It may be prayer for healing or provision, for study or relationships, or just a blessing. Most people I meet are open to prayer. I always ask permission and I don't push it. A lot of the people I talk to are under age so it's especially important to ask for their permission, gently and not forcibly.

## Story of Brook

I first met Brook in the winter of 2016 when I approached a group of about six girls sat together in the Mall. She was the eldest in the group, and the others obviously looked up to her. Brook seemed very dubious of me but I asked if I could share the Gospel with her and the other girls, and they all agreed.

About half way through, two more girls joined in who I'd met once before; that helped.

Later in the day I went to the park to meet up with some kids I knew well. Who should come along? Brook. It was getting cold and everyone was hungry, so I invited those that were hungry to have wedges and 'God-talk' at a local café. Brook came with a few others.

I've subsequently got to know Brook very well and I do have a soft spot for her. She has been through a lot and it's been great to get to know her, encourage her and share about Jesus with her. She will regularly text me to see if I'm in town and she'll often bring her friends to meet me too. We've had a lot of 'God-talk' and eaten a lot of wedges! Now, when we finish our time in a coffee shop Brook will tell any others that are with us that they can't go until I've prayed for them all.

One day in March 2017 we were sitting in a coffee shop and Brook got a phone call. I continued talking with the other kids there while she went off to talk on the phone. When she came back she was quite worked up. She had been falsely accused of something and someone was spreading rumours about her.

Normally she would have sworn a lot as she told us what was going on, but as I was there, she kept all but one swear word under her breath. I was very impressed.

## Street Ministry Protocol

As a ministry we do have a list of policies and procedures for evangelism. This is in keeping with changes in society and shows our diligence in doing everything wisely and legally. It also helps everyone to be on the same page; to reflect Jesus and so as to protect against any allegations of how we share the Gospel. As a ministry we also require people to have their Blue Card to do street ministry with us. This card is a thorough police check and allows people in Tasmania to work with children and vulnerable people.

## Story of Jack and Luke

During one of our free sausage sizzle events in the park in November 2015 I met Jack and Luke. They were in their late teens and very full-on young guys. They were also very open to the Gospel. When I asked if I could pray for them, Jack asked if I could pray for his eyes. He was continually squinting and it was very annoying to him. I prayed.

I didn't meet these guys again until March 2017. As I talked with them and a friend of theirs they just bombarded me with lots of questions. Could they be Christians if they had tattoos? Could they be Christians if they'd had sex? What about selling weed? And smoking weed? And what about getting drunk? I explained that no sin is so big that God can't forgive you if you repent and turn away from those sins. As I finished talking along came Abe who had broken some fingers. I prayed for him. Luke then wanted prayer for his Mum to be healed from Alzheimer's and then Jack spoke up that his eyes weren't squinty any more after that prayer at the sausage sizzle. Isn't God good? Jack and Luke said they'd come to church on Sunday, and sure enough, they kept their word, and rocked up about 50 minutes late. But they came.

In recent weeks I've seen a lot of Jack and Luke and we've had quite a few 'God-talks' and wedges. They both believe in God, and actually they're more open to Christianity than many others I've met. Luke especially, says that he believes in God, but he's not quite ready to be a Christian, as he says there's more sin he wants to do first! I see so much 'God' potential in these two young men. I trust it won't be long before they come into God's kingdom.

*"Be anxious for nothing, but in everything by prayer and supplication, with thanksgiving, let your requests be made known to God; and the peace of God, which surpasses all understanding, will guard your hearts and your minds through Christ Jesus."*

*Philippians 4:6-7*

*"The man who mobilizes the Christian church to pray will make the greatest contribution to world evangelization in history."*

*Andrew Murray*

## Chapter 6

# Prayer

## Preparation and Persistence Brings Revival

This book is primarily a book on evangelism so this chapter is not exhaustive of the subject of prayer but is more specifically about prayer for boldness, prayer for the lost, prayer for revival and prayer for those who are out sharing their faith.

In *1 Thessalonians 5:17* it says to pray without ceasing. God likes to hear our prayers. In *Matthew 6:6* it says to pray in secret, just you and the Lord. What is done in the secret place will affect what goes on in our public life. God is in the secret place and He hears us there. As we walk through each day in the Spirit, in God's presence, in an attitude of prayerfulness, be ready and attentive to what the Spirit is saying.

## Motives for Prayer

Some questions to ask yourself:

Am I praying to impress God or man? What is my motive when I pray?

Do I pray more when around others or when alone with God? Is my public prayer life an overflow of my private prayer life?

When I pray publicly, am I more concerned about what others think than what God thinks? Am I praying long prayers to look good to man? Aimless repetition is not necessary; God hears the first time. He already knows what we need before we ask.

## Preparation Prayer

Before going out to sow seeds of the Gospel, prepare the ground through prayer and fasting. We are in a post-Christian culture in Australia, which is very quickly becoming anti-Christian. The ground has been hardened, but the power of prayer is amazing. Pray for your family, your relatives, your friends, the people you work with, where you shop, the parks you visit, the gym you go to, the people you meet daily etc.

Every time we go into town we pray. We pray about the street ministry and who we will meet. We pray for Youth night and those who will come. We pray for our Sunday service for those who come, especially the lost, that they will have open hearts to receive the truth. In other words, you can't pray too much. People's eternal well-being is at stake. If we don't pray over the seeds sown, our enemy Satan is likely going to come and steal the seeds. We also pray after we've shared with people and we pray with people when they allow us. Pray, pray, pray, and then pray some more. This is serious business.

> *"Now this is the confidence that we have in Him, that if we ask anything according to His will, He hears us. And if we know that He hears us, whatever we ask, we know that we have the petitions that we have asked of Him." 1 John 5:14-15*

## Prayer for Compassion for the Lost

Taking time to pray for the lost, especially those we meet day after day, or those we have sown seeds of the Gospel into, comes from a heart of compassion. This compassion comes from Christ and is a work of the Holy Spirit in our lives. This compassion sees what the natural eye cannot see. It sees people heading towards eternity without God, towards eternal torment. Oh, that we would have a burden to pray for the lost and then be activated to go tell them of our wonderful God. It is God's mercy that we are in a season of grace, but we need to be sure we are praying and interceding and opening our mouths and preaching the Gospel. The days are evil and the time is short.

## Quotes from Andrew Murray

*"If there is one thing I think the Church needs to learn, it is that God means prayer to have an answer, and that it has not entered into the heart of man to conceive what God will do for His child who gives himself to believe that his prayer will be heard."*

*"Many complain that they have not the power to pray in faith, to pray the effectual prayer that avails much. The message I would bring to them is that the blessed Jesus is waiting, is longing, to teach them this. Christ is our life: in Heaven He ever lives to pray; His life in us is an ever-praying life, if we will but trust Him for it. Christ teaches us to pray not only by example, by instruction, by command, by promises, but by showing us Himself, the ever-living Intercessor, as our Life. It is when we believe this, and go and abide in Him for our prayer-life too, that our fears of not being able to pray aright will vanish, and we shall joyfully and triumphantly trust our Lord to teach us to pray, to be Himself the life and the power of our prayer."*

## God Moves in Answer to Our Prayers

God relented on destroying the children of Israel because of Moses' intercession and pleading with Him (*Exodus 32*). Also with the great city of Nineveh in the book of Jonah, God relented on destroying their city when the people cried out to Him and repented. That is, even in God's Sovereignty He has chosen us to be part of seeing change happen through our prayer and intercessions. Prayer is powerful, it requires faith and sometimes persistence, but we can see mountains moved through prayer.

Will you pray for boldness to preach the Gospel to the lost? Even though Peter and John got arrested for preaching Jesus, many believed (*Acts 4*), and they continued with even greater boldness. We can pray their same prayer for boldness too.

> *"Now, Lord, look on their threats, and grant to your servants that will all boldness they may speak your word, by stretching out Your hand to heal, and that signs and wonders may be done through the name of Your holy servant Jesus." Acts 4:29-30*

Will you pray that prayer today and believe that God will move in and through you? Will you pray and believe for a breakthrough today in your suburb, town or city? Even though you will be opposed by the works of Satan, don't be afraid.

Pray believing prayers for a move of God's Spirit as you ask for more boldness. Ask and believe and don't stop asking and believing until the breakthrough comes. In *Proverbs 28:1* it says, *"the wicked flees when no one pursues but the righteous are bold as a lion."* And in *Ephesians 6:19-20*, Paul asked for prayer for more boldness. Don't be content with where you're at, but be like the early disciples. Ask God for more boldness. I know I do. It may be to share the Gospel with one person at a time or it may be to share with a crowd. You will need boldness to stand up and proclaim the Gospel as our society moves from a post-Christian culture to an anti-Christian culture at a rapid rate.

## Ask and Believe

Pray often. Pray with sincerity of heart. Pray and pray again. Ask and keep on asking. It's present progressive tense. It's on going and it's persistent. Every one of us can ask. This wasn't just for the early disciples, but for all of us. A day-old Christian has the same privilege to ask of God anything in prayer just as much as a Christian of 40 years or more. It's about the faithfulness of God to answer, but it's also about our willingness to ask. God, being omniscient (all-knowing), knows what we need even before we ask but He has designed prayer to be the means to see things happen. Bring everything to God in prayer: your burden for the lost, your desire to see revival, your willingness to go and speak and even your fear to go and preach the Gospel. We can have no greater support than the Father because He's such a good Father. The more time you spend in communion with God, the more you will know what to ask for in accordance with God's will. Father God is especially concerned about the lost.

## Ask God

We can ask God for wisdom, protection, healing, faith, the lost, anything. He hears and answers prayer. His love, tenderness and goodness far exceeds that of any earthly parent. God is all knowing and He is infinitely wise so He knows what we need, what we desire and what is best for us. But He still desires that we ask.

So ask Him today for what it is you need. If we are asking for something that we think would be good for us but God knows that it won't be, He will protect us and give us what is best, that is, what is better. He knows what is good for us so we need to trust Him to do what is right for us. Our desire should be, "Father your will be done." Sometimes we unknowingly ask of God for something that will hurt us.

It is good to know He will not give us that which would be harmful or detrimental to us. If we have ignorantly or foolishly asked for something that would not be good for us, we can rest assured that our wise and loving Heavenly Father will deny us our request.

## Private Prayer

Jesus talked about prayer in *Matthew 6:6*;

> *"But you, when you pray, go into your room, and when you have shut your door, pray to your Father who is in the secret place, and your Father who sees in secret will reward you openly".*

Prayer is something we are called to do. It's not 'if' we pray but 'when' we pray. Prayers are powerful and God is motivated to act from our prayers. In *Luke 18:1* Jesus said that we always ought to pray and not lose heart. Make your prayers and requests known before God. God never tires of our prayers. He desires relationship with us and one of the ways to build a good relationship with anyone is through communication. God likes to hear us and He has told us to ask Him for what we need, like any good parent would do. Prayer is the appointed means for asking and receiving our petition from God.

It is important to pray daily, not just when you're at church or with other Christians. Remember prayer is two-way. We talk to God and we listen to what He has to say to us. For example my husband and I would not have a good relationship if only one of us talked and the other one only ever listened. A good relationship always requires both parties to talk and also to listen. This is the same in our relationship with God. We talk, God listens; God talks and we listen.

## Search Your Heart

While praying, it is always good to do a heart check. If we are to be lights shining in the darkness we need to be sure our hearts are right with God. Only then can we be sure our motives are pure and that everything we do is done in love, to glorify Jesus.

## Corporate Prayer

It's good to pray together with other believers. The prayer of agreement is powerful. It does not require a multitude to pray together, even just two is powerful.

> *"Again I say to you that if two of you agree on earth concerning anything that they ask, it will be done for them by My Father in Heaven. For where two or three are gathered together in My name, I am there in the midst of them."*
> *Matthew 18:19-20*

## Love Hobart prayer meeting stories

After the Rock café closed, we were blessed with the use of a council building for our Sunday meeting. As we settled in, we wondered what to do about our weekly prayer meeting as the council building we used for church was not available on a week night. We tried having a prayer meeting in someone's home a few suburbs away from the city but it didn't seem to be the right location. As we prayed about it, we sensed we should be praying near to where we were doing street ministry. We then started meeting on the Parliament lawns every Monday evening for an hour. Having an outdoor prayer meeting was a big step for us all and very uncomfortable for a few people from our church. As we persevered in corporate prayer, even though we had no building to use in the city, God blessed us. Oftentimes we braved the elements, looking like Eskimos, for our weekly prayer meeting but God was always there.

## A Drunk Guy and Our Prayer Meeting

One night we had just started praying when along came a 22 year old young guy who was quite drunk. I'd met him on street ministry once before when he was sober. He wanted to know what we were doing. I told him we were praying and I invited him to join us. We ended up praying a lot for him. He was hungry so we took him to Subway to feed him and then had some more prayer with him there. The Holy Spirit was touching him powerfully. He was overwhelmed by all the love. He kept crying as he sensed the presence of God. He was sober enough to remember his phone number and I rang the next day to check on him, and we had coffee together.

We've also seen fights break out nearby us as we've been praying, there have been streakers and then there were others who have seen us and come and joined the prayer meeting: Christians and non-Christians alike. Time and time again we've been driving to prayer meeting in the pouring rain and it stops raining just as we get to the park to pray. God is so good in looking after us.

## Story from Monday 6th February 2017

During prayer meeting tonight in the park, a group of 4 backpackers came and sat near us. So of course I shared the Gospel. They were so open. One from China needed a lift to the airport and the other three were going to camp in a tent up the mountain. We invited them to camp on our property as it was going to be a cold night and the mountain temperature was going to be close to zero degrees. You never know what a day will bring when you walk with Jesus. After the prayer meeting we dropped the girl from China at the airport having prayed with her and given her a Bible. She also really wanted an EvangeCube so I gave her a mini one to take with her. The other three backpackers; two from England and one from Mexico came back to our place to spend the night. It had seemed a bit crazy to invite them as the next day we were getting new carpets so we had furniture everywhere. They ended up sleeping in our family room on couches and a mattress. But that night six members of our family started vomiting! In the morning the backpackers helped me take apart beds and get everything downstairs for the carpets to go in upstairs, including moving all the sick ones and their buckets. I then spent 2 hours sharing my testimony with the backpackers and answering questions, before dropping them at the beach. They stayed an extra night so as to help move all the furniture back upstairs ready for the carpets going in downstairs the next day. We fed them and prayed with them. So God provided all we needed and all they needed!

## Persistent Prayer

Who likes waiting? Not many of us, I think. But in regard to salvations, as we wait for a move of God, we also need to be praying persistent prayers for the lost and for revival. It involves longevity; you must keep on going in the prayer closet. Never give up. Will you keep going against the odds? It may involve being in a battle for the lost souls of your city. Continue on in prayer in spite of outward circumstances, opposition from the devil or anything else. We need persistent determination in prayer while having thanksgiving in our heart.

## Finish Your Race Well

People often start well at something and that goes for evangelism too. Some people are so keen and enthusiastic at the start. But as time goes on they get weary as the initial excitement leaves. Evangelism is at times, just plain hard work. so even when the initial excitement wears off or when the going gets tough and you feel worn out: persevere. Press on, never giving up. Even if you FEEL like giving up at times, don't (*2 Corinthians 4:8-9*). Perseverance is needed and we can ask God to help us.

## Pray for Courage

If you feel you're lacking courage, pray to be filled with the Spirit as they did in *Acts 4:29-31*. They prayed for boldness, they were filled with the Spirit and then they spoke the Word of God with boldness (see Chapter 2). When you've done that, be ready and willing to preach the Gospel to whoever God brings across your path.

If you're not bold, pray for boldness, and if you're already bold, pray for more boldness. Pray for boldness for each other and for healings, signs and wonders to follow the preaching of the Word. Then see what God will do through you. If all God's people did this imagine what could happen? Revival and a breaking of the powers of darkness over the land. Revival sees strongholds of Satan defeated and a mighty harvest of souls into God's Kingdom. So get praying for boldness and expect God to move.

## Season of Planting

A planting season is hard, often there's very little fruit as it's not time for the harvest; it's too early. But the harvest will surely come as the seeds are being sown, because we know God's Word will not return to Him void. Will you hang in there for that? It's not easy. We can look around and think we're so small, so weak and we're working so hard. Where's the fruit? But we're still planting. The Bible shows us the principle of sowing and reaping. The farmer sows seed and then he waits. Seed does not grow over night. It takes time for the harvest to come in. So it is with us. It can take time to see the harvest come from sowing our seeds of the Gospel. But the harvest will come in due season if we don't give up.

*"Do not be deceived, God is not mocked; for whatever a man sows, that he will also reap. For he who sows to his flesh will of the flesh reap corruption, but he who sows to the Spirit will of the Spirit reap everlasting life. And let us not grow weary while doing good, for in due season we shall reap if we do not lose heart." Galatians 6:7-9*

I encourage you: don't give up because the harvest is coming. Are you ready for the harvest? When it comes there will be lots of change and we will all be busier than we are now. In the waiting season perseverant prayer is needed as well as preparation for the harvest. Also be patient. When the Holy Spirit is truly working in someone's life, there'll be no stopping them getting saved and the salvations will come. Ploughing up hard ground takes time, energy, resources, faith, commitment, and most of all love for the lost. Come into God's presence in prayer, to be encouraged and be expectant that He will move.

## Love Hobart update- 6th June 2016

Despite the very cold weather on Tuesday, I was able to share the Gospel with about 30 people. This included a concreter from Ulverstone, a guy studying journalism from Canada, a girl studying business/law and a 19 year old childcare worker who had a friend with anorexia who I prayed for and bound the spirit of anorexia (she'd been hearing voices). There was an atheist studying IT who was not very open but he still listened. Then there were a few different groups from Rosny and Elizabeth colleges, a lady from Taiwan who had a Christian sister and a lady from England. I saw a lady from Iraq sitting on a bench looking sad. I shared Jesus with her and prayed then went and bought her the Gospel of John in Arabic. Later I met up with three teenagers at a café for food and 'God-talk'. I prayed with them before we all headed to the park. As soon as we went round the corner to the park some of the kids saw me (it was nearly dark) and they called out my name and some of the girls came running down. There were about fifteen teens there altogether. There were three girls I hadn't met before.

One asked for a Bible as she'd seen her friends' Bibles. I shared the Gospel with her and the other two who said they'd heard about me. They wanted Bibles too and I prayed with them as well. After 7 hours in town in the freezing cold I was quite ready to go home but two of the girls were keen to talk more, so off to a coffee shop we went for food, 'God-talk' and prayer.

Friday was busy too but the highlight was talking to an atheist and his friend who had a catholic schooling background. I asked what led him to be an atheist and he said, "All the bad stuff in the world." I explained about the two spiritual kingdoms coming against each other and how Satan hates mankind and God loves mankind etc. It was like the lights went on for him and he and his friend were then both keen for a Bible and prayer. Later in the park one kid wanted to have prayer for her sins which she wanted to confess and then some of the others did too. That was a precious moment as these kids never would have thought about their sins before I met them. Then at Youth we had lots of kids and lots of fun. On Saturday we had two teens come over to our place to hang out with my kids and we had an awesome time with them. More street ministry training on Saturday afternoon. The highlight was sharing the Gospel with a French girl who was an atheist and later confessed she was a lesbian. She took two different tracts and allowed us to pray for her.

## The Power of Prayer Leading into Revival

My hope for everyone reading this book is that prayer becomes a big part of your lifestyle, if it hasn't already. I know I can only do what I do because I spend time in God's presence praying. What a blessing to commune with the God who created us; to know Him intimately and to have Him reveal His heart to us; to know He loves us to pray to Him.

Praying for the lost is a forerunner to revival. Revival is a term that generally refers to a specific time of increased spiritual activity in the life of a church or churches, either regionally or globally. We are praying for revival in our city and it's helpful to look at how revivals have come in the past. One key element is prayer. That is, heartfelt, persistent prayer for a move of God.

## The Welsh Revival

God worked especially through Evan Roberts to start the Welsh revival. He was a young man of prayer, full of passion for Jesus and a burden for the lost. Prayer was a hallmark of this revival. Another feature of this revival that was not seen in any other revival prior to 1904 was the role of the media. The daily newspapers spread news of conversions and generated an air of excitement about the revival that helped to fuel it further.

The revival spread to Scotland and England, with estimates that a million people were converted in Britain. Missionaries subsequently carried the revival spirit abroad; it was especially influential on the Pentecostal movement in the USA.

## Azusa Street Revival

This revival started through prayer meetings in a home in 1906 in a poor suburb of Los Angeles. As the house filled up with people day after day, an old warehouse in Azusa Street was then leased. Meetings happened day and night with preaching, prayer and worship. On a number of occasions the fire brigade were called as the building appeared to be on fire. This revival continued to 1915. It was the start of the modern day Pentecostal movement in the USA and it was initially influenced by the Welsh revival.

## The Hebrides Revival 1949

The Hebrides is a group of islands to the north west of Scotland. Duncan Campbell was invited to hold evangelical meetings that met with resistance even from local Christians and only seven initially came to his meetings. Then one night they went to a farm house to fast and pray. As one young man prayed, especially regarding the people having clean hands and pure hearts the house started shaking and the dishes started rattling. Outside people came running and asking about Jesus. This was the beginning of the Hebrides revival. A 15 year old boy who was saved became a frontline prayer warrior. Age is never a barrier to God. Two sisters in their eighties had prayed for years for revival. Again prayer was a key to this revival.

## The Indonesian Revival 1965

This revival started in a Presbyterian church where everything in the service was planned and written down beforehand, with no room for change. On this particular day the people in the meeting all heard a rushing mighty wind like a tornado, but nothing was moving. Then the fire bell across the street at the police station rang, and the policeman saw the church was on fire. But it wasn't a natural fire, it was the fire of God. Many were convicted and saved and baptised in the Spirit that night, and though the meeting started with 200 people it finished with a 1000, as people came running from all over town to see what was going on. A new convert then stood up, preached and told everyone they were to go out and preach the Gospel. The next day many went out preaching the Gospel from village to village, with signs following them.

## Prayer and Passion for the Lost

Past revivals have started from people praying together, not just praying alone. The desire to be in the Fathers presence becomes so strong. It's like people cannot help but pray. Didn't that happen at Pentecost? They all spoke at the same time.

The Spirit gave them utterance all at once. It happened in the Indonesian revival too. We must not be limited by our preconceived ideas of what we think is right or not, but we must let the Spirit lead. Along with preparing the ground for revival through prayer there needs to be a passion, even an urgency to see souls saved. Immediately after the Spirit came at Pentecost, Peter preached the Gospel boldly. Will you spend time praying and weeping for the lost? Ask the Lord to ignite the fire of your heart for the lost. They are falling into Hell which is a place of eternal torment. Will you pray?

## Man Cannot Start A Revival—Only God Can

We need the fire of God to come on us. In *Acts 2:47* it says the Lord added to the church daily. That is, it was His work. The Lord will send the fire of revival when He sees fit, not when we see fit. It will come whether it is convenient to us or not, whether we're busy or tired, whether we're ready or not. Will we accept God's revival fire no matter what, no matter when?

We need a wave of Godly fear to come to our nation. We desperately need revival, to see God glorified and to stop the godlessness that is increasing. A God-given burden is needed concerning the lost and on-going prayer must become a priority if we are to see revival.

## Who Does God Use To Start Revival?

Ordinary people, just like you and me who have been faithful in the ordinary and faithful in prayer. Revival will bring persecution to those God uses to start it. There will be those that mock as there were at Pentecost. But don't fear man, fear God alone and rejoice and give thanks in everything. The temptation may be to try to defend yourself, but that can end up being a distraction. You need to keep your hand to the plough and not be distracted by tactics of the enemy to try to get your eyes, heart and mind off God's work.

## Do You Want Revival To Come?

Revivals don't usually look like what we expect. In fact, many people that pray for revival don't like it when it actually comes. When God brings revival fire through the Holy Spirit, He chooses how that looks. Expect the unexpected. At Pentecost they didn't know how long they would have to wait until the Holy Spirit came and they had no idea what that would look like. Are you ready to be uncomfortable? It will mean change. It will mean getting out of your comfort zone. To be used by God will cost you everything. Are you willing to stand out and be different because of your passion for Jesus? Others won't like it. You'll be called names, but there will be a cloud of witnesses in Heaven cheering you on. Be willing to live like Jesus, to be on-fire and passionate, to love the lost and love even your enemies. May God raise up radicals, the fearless men and women of God who are willing to be different. Satan isn't worried about lukewarm Christians, he's only worried about those who are on fire for Jesus. He will send conflict, but you will be at peace with God as you obey Him.

## Revival Doesn't Come Cheap

There is always a cost to a revival. A revival generally only comes when we are ready to sacrifice everything for it. Are you willing to let God take you out of your comfort zone? Are you willing to give God all of you? When you truly know Him, it isn't so hard. He is worth giving up anything and everything for.

Following Jesus will always involve sacrifice. I don't know about you but I don't want to just be an ordinary Christian that lives an ordinary life. I want to live an abundant life in Jesus through the power of the Holy Spirit. I want to do great exploits for God. I live in expectation of God moving more and more in me as I say, "Here I am Lord use me."

Pray that the fire of God is ignited in your belly. Pray that the Father revives you. Spend time aside with the Father as Jesus did.

Pray that we will see Hell plundered and Heaven filled for Jesus. Will you get on your knees and pray for mercy? Stop using the intellect to overcomplicate the Bible and get back to the simplicity of it. Obey God, believe His Word—all of it! Allow the Holy Spirit to have control of every area of your life. And remember, we get trained in the ordinary. God uses ordinary people to do supernatural works. Ask God for a fresh hunger for more of Him. There is so much more that God wants to reveal to us than what we already know. Be expectant for a move of God. Do you want to see a rushing mighty wind of God and the fire of God come out of your inner most being? Then be ready and willing to lay your life down inobedience.

## A Personal Prayer for Revival

"Father, Your Word says we will do greater works than Jesus. Our city/town /suburb has been a dry place spiritually and according to Your Word I pray that You will come and water this dry and thirsty land: that You will send Your revival fire. I pray Your Kingdom come to this land and that Your will be done, that You would move in might and power. Prepare me and show me anything in me that needs to be put right, whatever there is Lord and then Father send Your revival fire I pray. Amen."

The outcome of a true revival has always been a renewed conviction of sin and repentance, followed by an intense desire to live in obedience to God. It is giving up one's own will to do God's will. John Wesley described revival as a people saturated with God. Andrew Murray writes:

*"As each of us pleads for revival throughout the church, let us also cry to God for our own neighbourhood or sphere of work. Let there be great searching in*

*the heart of every minister and lay worker as to whether they are ready to give such time and strength to prayer as God would have. Just as in public they are leaders of their larger or smaller circles, let them in secret take their places in front rank of the great intercessory host. They must prevail with God before revival and floods of blessing can come. Of all who speak of, think of, or long for revival, let not one hold back in this great work of honest, earnest, specific pleading. Revive your work, O Lord! Will you not revive us again?"*

*"But you shall receive power when the Holy Spirit is come upon you; and you shall be witnesses to Me in Jerusalem, and in all Judea and Samaria, and to the end of the earth."*

*Acts 1:8*

*"In other words, every Spirit-filled believer has a potential capacity for every gift of the Spirit, they are not the purview of a privileged few. That idea is confirmed by Paul's careful statement, "there are varieties of gifts, but the same Spirit". His emphasis does not fall upon possession of the gifts but upon possession of the Holy Spirit who is the source of all gifts."*

*Ken Chant*

## Chapter 7

# Gifts of the Spirit in Evangelism

## The Power of God

We read throughout the New Testament about the gifts of the Holy Spirit called the 'charismata'. In *1 Corinthians 12:1-12* there is a list of nine specific gifts the Holy Spirit releases in the body of Christ. There are three gifts of revelation: word of wisdom, word of knowledge and discerning of spirits. There are three gifts of power: gift of faith, gift of healings and the working of miracles. Then there are three gifts of utterance: prophecy, tongues and the interpretation of tongues. The early church lived and moved in these supernatural gifts. We read in *Acts 10* that the gift of the Holy Spirit was also poured out on the Gentiles. When you receive the baptism of the Holy Spirit you also receive gifts of the Holy Spirit, as the Spirit wills. They are available to all Christians, not just a few (reference Ken Chant).

## What about the Gifts Today?

The gifts of the Spirit did not end with the apostles. How do we know? That which is perfect has not come (*1 Corinthians 13:10-12*). As Ken Chant (1995) says:

*"The perfection referred to by Paul is certainly the perfected church — but it is equally certainly not the early church as such. Commentators of every persuasion are happily agreed that Paul is talking about the perfection the church will attain when the church is finally glorified in Heaven"*

When that happens we won't need the gifts. In the meantime though, we should not despise or reject the things God gives us, but rather embrace them.

There is much evidence today of tongues, prophecies, faith and the other gifts operating through God-fearing, Bible-believing Christians who are walking in obedience to God. Yes, there is the fake too, and we do need to be on guard against wolves, imposters and the like. That is why we are to test the spirit behind what is said.

*"Do not quench the Spirit. Do not despise prophecies. Test all things, hold fast what is good." 1 Thessalonians 5:19-21*

When Jesus walked the earth, He led by example. He demonstrated the love of the Father through the power of the Holy Spirit. He preached, He healed the sick, He raised the dead and cast out demons. In the Great Commission in *Mark 16* He commanded us to go do the same.

*"And He (Jesus) said to them, 'Go into all the world and preach the Gospel to every creature. He who believes and is baptised will be saved; but he who does not believe will be condemned. And these signs will follow those who believe: In My name they will cast out demons, they will speak with new tongues; they will take up serpents; and if they drink anything deadly, it will by no means hurt them; they will lay hands on the sick, and they will recover.'*
*"Mark 16:15-18*

We are to boldly do the works of Jesus while walking in our God-given authority. We are to be ready to preach the Gospel, heal the sick and cast our demons, while not being concerned about outcomes. You might wonder what if they're not healed or delivered and I will look stupid? Only be concerned about being obedient to God. The outcome is God's business.

## The Gifts of the Spirit

The gifts are a blessing to be used to glorify the Lord. The gifts of the Spirit are given as God wills *(1 Corinthians 12:11)*. The manifestations of the Spirit are for the profit of all. In *1 Corinthians 12: 4-7* it says it is the One and the same Holy Spirit that gives diversities of gifts, with differences of ministries and diversities of activities. They are still in operation today all around the world, and we have seen them too.

For example, one day about 7 years ago as I was speaking in tongues I had the interpretation that I would be a, 'Mother-Pastor.' I didn't really know what that meant, or what that would look like, but 7 years down the track it perfectly describes my role with the youth of Hobart.

Another example, this time in relation to prophecy. In 2014 I sensed the Holy Spirit saying we would run something like a drop-in lounge for the youth of Hobart. That was about a year before we started Youth which is really like a drop-in lounge.

An example of the gift of faith would be when we started the Rock café. We didn't have the money or resources but God did it anyway. The gift of faith believes what is impossible in the natural.

The gifts need to be used under the guidance of the Holy Spirit whether in church or on the streets. When people try to force the gifts they may well be opening up to demonic manifestations, so again, test if it is the Spirit of God. There are counterfeit spirits as Satan has supernatural power and can disguise himself as an angel of light. For example, on the streets we have people who ask us to give them a prophetic word. We'll pray and ask

God, but we only prophesy if the Spirit gives us a prophecy. Don't feel pressured to give a word when you haven't actually received one.

## Testimony

One evening Joanne and I walked through the Mall. We saw Amanda sitting by herself. She was only 14 years old but we knew her well, as she was often in town. We sat down and had a chat with her and prayed for her broken arm. A few minutes later her friend Naomi arrived followed shortly after by Gemma and Shane. Shane had a Christian background and as we talked he asked if we could prophesy over him. I said we were happy to pray for him, but we could only give him a prophecy if the Lord gave us one for him. So Joanne and I prayed and we did get a prophecy for him. We then asked the other kids if they would like us to pray for them as well which they all happily agreed to. As we continued praying with them we could sense the presence of God in a very powerful way and it became obvious the kids were sensing this too. Naomi started to get agitated so I went and sat next to her. She was coming under conviction of sin and she knew she was not fit for Heaven. As I talked quietly with her about salvation, Joanne continued to pray and prophesy over the others. As Joanne started praying for Gemma she sensed that she had a broken heart. This was the first time we'd met Gemma so we didn't know anything about her. Gemma said to Joanne, "How did you know?" Joanne told her that she sensed that was what God was saying. Gemma said, "Yes I do have a broken heart.

My boyfriend just broke up with me." One outcome that night was that Naomi went straight home to be by herself, instead of going to a party with the others.

## Desire God-Given Gifts

We should desire spiritual gifts as evidence of the Holy Spirit dwelling in us, and so we can be a greater blessing to others by showing them the power of God. We don't just have to desire the lesser gifts, but prophecy and the best gifts as it says in *1 Corinthians 12:31*. We must also be sure to glory in the Lord and not the gifts. Your desire to prophesy should be so you can build people up. Your desire for a gift of healing should be so you can see people set free from afflictions of the flesh, not to make yourself feel important which comes from a root of pride. The gifts of the Holy Spirit enable us to do things we could not naturally do, like prophesying and healing.

## How Many Gifts does God Give One Person?

The Bible doesn't say. What we do know is this; he who is faithful with little will be given more. God blesses faithfulness and obedience. In the parable of the talents in *Matthew 25:14- 30* we read of three servants who were each given talents. One was given five, another two, and the other was given one. The warning here is for the one who thinks he doesn't have much, then doesn't use the little he has. Be faithful with what you already have whether little or much. As you're faithful with what you already have, you never know what God will give you next.

## The Gifts Confirm the Message of Truth

God says He will confirm the preaching of His Word with signs and wonders (*Mark 16:20, Hebrews 2:1-4*). We need to walk in faith, preach the Word and expect God to release gifts. People may see miracles, but we must remember it is the hearing of the Word that brings men to repentance. In the story of the rich man and Lazarus (*Luke 16:19-31*), the rich man pleaded with Father Abraham to send Lazarus back from the dead to warn his brothers of the eternal torment they were heading towards. But Abraham said if they rejected Moses and the Prophets, they would not be persuaded even if a dead person was to rise from the dead.

## God is Still Giving Gifts of the Spirit

We are filled with the Spirit so that we might magnify the Lord Jesus Christ, like on the day of Pentecost, and like Cornelius and his household and many others in the Bible. We are given gifts of the Spirit so God may be glorified through us. Being a Christian is not boring as some may think. When you operate in the gifts and power of the Spirit, life sure won't be boring. As you earnestly expect the best gifts, desire to be so full of God that the gifts of the Spirit operating through you will always glorify the Lord.

## Healing Evangelism

Can God trust you with a gift of healing? Would you give Jesus all the glory or would you take some glory for yourself? The gift of healing is nothing to do with us but everything to do with Jesus. It's all about Him. When there is unbelief and worldliness in the Church these gifts of healing are not very evident. Humility is a key here. We need to be sure not to think more highly of ourselves than we ought. God chooses whom He wills. At all times we need to humbly remember that all that we are and all that we do is because of the grace of God on our lives. It is by faith in the name of Jesus that healing comes. Of ourselves we are nothing, we are powerless, but by God's grace through faith, we walk in the Spirit. It's all about Him. If you're lacking faith or walking in unbelief in the area of healing, get into your Word. Read the Gospels, read the book of Acts and let the Holy Spirit speak to you. Healing is all through the Bible in both the Old and New Testaments.

## Stories from the Streets

Amanda had her arm out of plaster not long after we prayed for her in the Mall, but she didn't have full movement. Next time we met her I held her arm and prayed for full movement to return to her arm and it did there and then. Apparently even her doctor was amazed that Amanda could move her arm fully next time she saw him.

On another occasion, Joanne and I ended up sitting in my car with three teens who were freezing cold as they weren't wearing much clothing. We spent an hour with them and the Holy Spirit moved powerfully. We prayed and prophesied over them and they were amazed. Interestingly, I had prayed for one of these girls for healing from bulimia about 3 weeks earlier and she told me that night that she hadn't thrown up since I prayed and she was enjoying eating again. Praise God!

I often get kids coming up to me to tell me they have been healed by God from a prayer we prayed. That is always exciting to hear as often I pray for healing and I don't see anything initially. We have heard of and seen many healings.

## Prophetic Evangelism

Prophecy is a message inspired by God that can be a revelation, instruction or telling of the future that you wouldn't know otherwise. It is God speaking through a person to reveal something from His heart. The primary focus of prophecy is encouragement, and may include words of knowledge.

Prophecy and words of knowledge are gifts of the Holy Spirit. As God's sheep we all have the ability to hear God's voice. To grow in the prophetic it is helpful to have a desire to hear God and then be ready, alert and listening to what the Holy Spirit would like to say to you. He may well release prophetic gifts or words of knowledge to you, but it is God that gives these gifts, we can't make them come. The Lord will give the gifts as He sees fit.

## How Do You Prophesy?

It's a gift from God, like healing, you can only do it as the Holy Spirit manifests through you. But we are to desire it, so you can ask God to give you a gift of prophecy *(1 Corinthians 14:1)*.

Spend time with the Lord and learn to hear His voice. This often comes with an inner witness. For example, it could be one word that comes into your thoughts. An example I had of this a few years ago was for my friend Debbie. She had come on board with us with the ministry of Love Hobart and the word 'stalwart' dropped into my spirit. I didn't really know the full meaning of it as it's not a word I use, but as I looked up the dictionary definition it so accurately described Debbie.

Sometimes a word of knowledge comes through sensing how someone is feeling as you talk to them; that can be the Holy Spirit alerting you to what the other person is going through.

I've sensed grief and rejection from different people and when I've asked if that's what they're going through it's turned out to be a word of knowledge. I've had this happen on the streets on quite a few occasions.

Prophecy can also come through dreams and visions, even showing you where to go to find people who need to hear the Gospel. Interpretation of tongues can also include prophecy.

## How Do You Grow In Prophecy?

From growing in your ability to hear God which comes from intimacy with God and expecting God to speak to you. My husband talks to me because he loves me and we have a good relationship. God loves me too and I know He likes to speak to me and share His heart. Position yourself to hear God. Get to know Him. Start with the Word which is a love letter to us from the Lord and it is also our foundation. Then learn to be sensitive to the still, small voice of the Holy Spirit, which comes from a life of obedience.

A love for the truth is crucial in discerning true prophecies from the false. The Holy Spirit is the Spirit of truth (*John 16:13*). You will need to know the Scriptures to know if a prophecy lines up and is truly a word from the Lord. The Bible is full of prophecy. It's a living Word. God still speaks through it today. In the last days we are warned there will be much deception. We need a love for the truth like never before. Jesus is the truth.

## Hindrances to Being Accurate In Prophecy

*Sin*-God didn't speak to Eli in *1 Samuel* because of sin in his family that he should have dealt with. God chose to speak through Samuel a young boy instead. Repent of sin.

*Being Unteachable*- learn to listen to correction, whilst walking in humility. Repent of any pride.

*Being Unavailable*- or too busy to take time to listen and build your relationship with Jesus. Be still, and get to know Him.

*Unbelief*- just not believing God will speak to you. Our relationship with God is two-way. God is still speaking. He wants you to hear His voice. Only believe!

## Dangers of the Prophetic

Prophecy can be abused but don't use that as an excuse to deny or despise prophecy. There is a warning in *1 Thessalonians 5:20* to not despise prophecy as previously quoted. Yes, there are many false prophets and false prophecies but don't let that harden you. Be willing to test prophecy but don't despise all prophecy because of a bad experience. When prophesying be careful NOT to say, "God told me this" or "God told me that." It is better to say, "This is what I believe God is saying..." There are Christians that say God spoke to them and told them to do things that are not Biblical. Do not use God as an excuse for justifying sin or what your flesh wants.

Some people just want a prophetic word to pamper their carnal desires, to tickle their ears, or to make them feel good. They go running after prophecies instead of seeking first God's kingdom. They never change or grow up or walk in obedience. God will give you a prophecy if He decides you need one. And if you move in the prophetic don't be pressured to give a false prophecy when you haven't received anything from God.

## How to Protect From False Prophecy

Test everything and hold fast to the truth. A true prophecy will bear witness to Jesus.

*'The testimony of Jesus is the spirit of prophecy.' Revelation 19:10*

Always be accountable. Satan is sneaky and can disguise himself as an angel of light. Always check: does the prophecy line up with the Word of God? True prophecy will never contradict the Word. Does it reveal the heart of the Father? He is full of compassion and mercy, but also a God of justice. Be teachable and correctable, whether giving a prophecy or receiving one. Be humble and submissive to God and His delegated authority. Learn to hear God in the secret place as you grow in your personal relationship with the Lord

## Evangelism Focus

Remember the focus with evangelism needs to be preaching the power of the cross. God says signs and wonders will follow the preaching of the Word. We should not be surprised if we see God move supernaturally after we have preached the Gospel.

## Faith

Step out in faith. Learn as much as you can from others. I wasn't an evangelist when I started sharing the Gospel but God has now given me the gift of evangelism. Obedience often comes first. In our society it's so easy to have back up plans for everything and avoid walking by faith, even in sharing the Gospel. This is not pleasing to God. It is faith that pleases God, not backup plans. Can God be trusted? Yes, always. Does He always move when we want Him to? No, He will move in His perfect time, even if it doesn't seem perfect to us. Will it be easy to share the Gospel? Not always, but if we are to obey God we need to be willing to open our mouths and share Jesus. Will you trust Him no matter what? My experience is I have at times felt stretched beyond measure but I'm still here, still trusting the Lord. The Lord is still growing my faith. I'm a work in progress. Out of a radical faith in God, radical boldness will come forth.

We will all have different gifts but we should expect God to speak to us- we're His sheep. Be alert and attentive to God speaking to you and have an expectation that He will speak. God hasn't stopped talking. To hear Him more clearly:

1. Check your heart for any unconfessed sin.
2. Know the Word. Start by reading it daily.
3. Pray. Get in your prayer closet daily and pray with others.
4. Walk in love and obedience. This comes from a relationship with God as you keep His commandments.
5. Keep a heart of thanksgiving and praise.

*"By this My Father is glorified, that you bear much fruit; so you will be My disciples."*

*John 15:8*

*"Let us not glide through this world and then slip quietly into Heaven, without having blown the trumpet loud and long for our Redeemer, Jesus Christ. Let us see to it that the devil will hold a thanksgiving service in Hell, when he gets the news of our departure from this field of battle called earth."*

*C.T. Studd*

# Chapter 8

# Fruit that remains

## Discipleship, Training Others & Multiplication

## Discipleship

After the command to 'GO', Jesus says:

*'Go therefore and make disciples of all the nations ...' Matthew 28:19*

Sharing the Gospel is closely related with the making of disciples. A disciple is one who accepts Jesus as Lord and Saviour and then assists in the spreading of the Gospel. That is, a disciple is proactive. You cannot be a disciple and do nothing. Being a disciple means you are growing in Jesus while being equipped by the Holy Spirit. Good discipleship comes from being discipled by someone who is further along the road in their journey with Jesus than you are: someone who has good fruit and reflects Jesus. Disciples will copy their disciple makers. It's a bit like the game 'follow the leader,' so disciple makers need to be a true reflection of Jesus. We imitate Jesus and then those around us can imitate us.

*"Imitate me, just as I also imitate Christ." 1 Corinthians 11:1*

Even a young or new disciple can make disciples. Look at the man in the tombs who was demon possessed and Jesus set Him free *(Mark 5:1-20)*. Immediately Jesus sent Him out to evangelise his neighbourhood.

To be a disciple we need to believe in Jesus as Lord and Saviour and be obedient to God. You can't be a disciple until you believe in Jesus, although I will say that a lot of what I am doing on the streets of Hobart looks like discipleship, even though the young ones aren't saved yet.

To be obedient to God we need to live by the Word in the power of the Spirit. Obedience to God is essential to become like Jesus.

> *"And being found in appearance as a man, He (Jesus) humbled Himself and became obedient to the point of death of the cross.' Philippians." 2:8*

## Get Ready to Disciple

We can't go and make disciples unless we are first ready and willing to share the Gospel. As you learn to share the Gospel, you will notice that your children learn too and others around you. That's Discipleship!

In *Romans 10:14-15* we read that people need to hear the preaching of the Gospel. If they don't hear the Gospel they cannot believe and be saved. As Disciples of Jesus Christ we need to be able to share the Gospel, the message of repentance and the power of the cross, Christ crucified and resurrected for us.

It seems to me a lot of Christians struggle in being able to share their faith. Can you explain the basis of your faith in Christ Jesus? Do you understand the word SUBSTITUTE? How are you going to grow in your ability to share the Gospel? Get around someone who can do it. That is, humble yourself and ask for help, then be teachable. Then be willing to learn. You can do online training or classroom training but when all is said and done it's not until you actually get out and share the Gospel that you really learn.

## Example of How NOT to Disciple

"God loves you and has a wonderful plan for your life. Say this prayer with me - now you're a Christian. You'll be right now. See you later."

What's wrong with this? There's no repentance, and so it is impossible to disciple them! Without a desire to repent there is no desire to change or be discipled. The desire to be discipled starts with the 'true' Gospel and that includes the need to repent and put Jesus first. Many people think they're saved because they said a prayer, maybe even years ago, but they never repented and they never allowed Jesus to be Lord of their lives. The way is narrow that leads to life, don't forget that. There is a cost to being a Christian. You no longer have rights. Your only right is obedience and surrender to the living God to do His will.

## Example of How to Disciple

"We are all sinners. We cannot go to Heaven in the strength of our own goodness. We will never be good enough. We need a redeemer. Someone who can be a substitute for us and His name is Jesus. He died on the cross in our place. We need to repent and put Jesus first in our lives."

When someone has accepted Jesus as their Lord and Saviour, they are ready to be discipled, and that includes training in how to share the Gospel. If you're not sharing the Gospel how are you going to teach others how to share it?

## Example of Discipling

A couple of years ago my friend Bronte invited me to go to a conference with her. I suggested instead of spending all that money that we use those three days to pray and share the Gospel. I was willing to teach Bronte everything I knew. We did spend those three days together doing just that. It was a precious time but also a productive time. Bronte first observed how I shared the Gospel with a few different people. After she'd observed me she had a go with me right there to help if she got stuck. Then she was ready to do it herself. It's always encouraging to equip someone to share the Gospel and impart the passion to do it. As Ben Armacost says, "Evangelism is caught more than taught."

## Steps of a Disciple after Conversion:

### 1. Baptism

Baptism is a command, not an option. It is an outward sign of obedience at the outset of your new life in Christ. Jesus Himself was baptised (*Matt 3:13-17*). Why was He baptised? He led by example and also fulfilled all righteousness. For someone to be ready for baptism, they need to have heard the Gospel, repented of their sins (*Acts 2:38*), and accepted Jesus as Lord and Saviour. The early church baptised as soon as people were saved (*Acts 16:30-33*). Don't put this off. Baptism is an identification with Jesus in His death, burial and resurrection. The Greek word 'baptizo' stems from the Greek word 'bapto' which means to dip. Baptism then is to be totally immersed (*Romans 6:3-4*). Baptism is symbolic of us dying to our flesh. We are buried with Jesus, then we are raised with Him to walk in newness of life in the Spirit. To be baptized is to declare, "I no longer live for myself but for Christ." It is a public declaration that I am now a child of God and it is a commitment to discipleship.

### 2. Teaching and Training in the Word

This is teaching based on the Word of God. Today we see teaching that caters for itchy ears with pop psychology, motivational messages or a watered down message of the Gospel and no mention of repentance.

We must not be afraid to preach the true Gospel, including consequences of sin, Hell and eternal separation from God. It is not a popular message but it is the truth. The New Testament teachings and doctrine are not old and outdated. They're liberating. And it is the truth that sets people free. Even on the day of Pentecost they preached Christ crucified and resurrected. Jesus disciples didn't preach, "I've had this amazing experience you should have it too." We don't need to find a different message. Jesus the Word made flesh, came to set us free. The power of the Gospel is still the same today. We can share testimony. We can pray and believe for miracles and healings but unless the Gospel is preached how can one believe and be saved?

Warning: don't just be a hearer of good teaching but be a doer too. Let the teaching of the Word sink into your spirit and then live it. Without a change in us, hearing good teaching is of no effect. You could have the best disciple maker in the world training you but unless you are willing to learn, change and grow it will be to no avail. Be ready and willing to hear and then to change, to be conformed into the image of Jesus.

## 3. Walking in the Spirit

Walking in the Spirit includes prayer, fasting, and giving, which are Christian disciplines that Jesus said we should follow in His Sermon on the Mount. The Sermon on the Mount in *Matthew 5, 6* and *7* is a good place to start training and teaching new disciples as this is really a great summary of the Christian life. Also *Acts 2:42 which reads:*

> *"And they continued steadfastly in the apostles' doctrine and fellowship, in the breaking of bread, and in prayers."*

Walking in the Spirit also includes walking in holiness. That is, fleeing sin while pursuing God.

## Keys for Disciple Makers

*Live by Example.* That is, don't just talk about Jesus but live like Jesus. If you know it in your head but you're not living it, there's a problem. It won't take long for someone to pick up what you're really like. Don't be a hypocrite for Jesus, be a disciple maker for Jesus. It will cost you. When you're discipling someone, they will see your strengths and weaknesses; you can't hide anything. But if there's wilful sin, that's not Ok.

Search your heart daily to deal with sin. Don't let sin take root.

Some years ago I led Millie to the Lord. She then came to my home for Bible study every week for 2 years. I was laying a foundation with her. She got to know me and my family well, and learnt a lot from 'doing life with us.' She later became a prison chaplain, and studied to be a pastor.

*Know Jesus, the Living Word.* If you don't know Jesus well, how can you imitate Him? Then how will you be an example to others? People who know each other well will often copy each other without realising. They'll start saying similar words, even their mannerisms can become similar. So be careful who you are hanging out with because you will imitate them. The best example of this is of a couple that have been married a long time. They become very similar.

It's not necessarily about how many disciples you make. Are you making disciples out of the one or two around you? Jesus spent 3 years training His disciples. Their big test came when He was arrested and they all scattered. But by the time of His ascension into Heaven these disciples were ready to make disciples, they received the Holy Spirit and they changed the world.

## The Great Commission

*Matthew 28:19* says, *"Go into all the world and make disciples"*. That's for all of us. Yes, some will be called to make many disciples and others only one or two. It's going to start with the one in front of you. Are you being faithful with the one(s) God has given you to disciple? Are you willing to lead? Who has God put in front of you to train, equip, prepare?

Discipleship takes time and commitment, but it's what we're called to do: all of us. It may only be one person but don't underestimate the power of discipling one. You never know if that one you're sowing into could change a nation. God, the Good Shepherd cares about the one. It's not always about multitudes of people. Discipleship is time and labour intensive. Are you willing? But more than that are you ready? Are you prepared? Are you walking with Jesus 24/7 or only when you think you're being watched? Being a disciple maker is not for wimps. But it's not for hypocrites either. Get your act together. Get ready and then be willing and available for Jesus. It won't always be easy but there will be many blessings along the way as you see the one(s) you're discipling grow and blossom and flourish.

It is interesting to note that Jesus, the Son of God, only had twelve disciples. Why? Why no more? Discipleship takes time and effort. Of those twelve, one was a traitor. Judas spent all that time with Jesus and knew Him intimately, yet betrayed Him. Why? Because he allowed Satan to fill his heart.

Sometimes you can sow a lot of time and energy into one person and they still may choose to let Satan fill their heart. But remember this happened to Jesus. People make choices every day. Jesus was the perfect disciple maker yet there was a traitor in His midst. As we follow in Jesus footsteps this may happen to us too. It's sad when that happens but we must not give up. Our time is God's time. Have we been faithful?

Outcomes are not our business, but faithfulness and obedience are. Will you be a good example of Christ?

## Disciple Making in the Home

Disciple making starts in the home. Parents disciple children.

*"My son give me your heart, And let your eyes observe my ways."*
*Proverbs 23:26*

Then it goes out from there. You're never too young to make disciples.
When our son Joseph was 8 or 9 years old I remember seeing him sat at a
table at the Rock sharing with a boy about baptism. That was a blessing
to see his willingness to do that. When our daughter, Shalom, was 7 years
old, she had a dream about sharing the Gospel and she's able to do
that very well by herself and she's only now 10 years old. She has really
captured the vision of the Great Commission. One Thursday when she
was 9 years old she used the EvangeCube all by herself to share the
Gospel with a shop assistant she'd gotten to know in the Mall. The lady
took a Bible and tract too.

This is so encouraging as Shalom is so young and it was her initiative
to want to share the Gospel. She had asked us all at our church prayer
meeting to pray that there would be an opportunity for her.

## Are You Ready to be a Disciple Maker?

If you're not ready, get ready. Get right with God. Deal with any sin. We
must live what we preach or our words become empty and meaningless.
Like Paul, we need to be ready to say, "come imitate me as I imitate
Christ." To make disciples we need to be a disciple. To be a disciple we
need to be obedient to God. To be obedient to God we need to live by
the Word in the power of the Spirit. So go make disciples, then be ready
to make more disciples, baptising them in the name of the Lord and
teaching them to obey Jesus' commandments.

## Testimony

I often get people saying to me that it's easy for me to share the Gospel because I'm an evangelist and I'm gifted in evangelism. But it wasn't always that way. I didn't always have the gift of evangelism, that's only come recently. Anointing comes from God but obedience is required of us often before we see any evidence of anointing. By faith, we open our mouths to preach the Gospel.

After watching the Way of the Master DVD series in 2008 I just knew I was to actively pursue obeying the Great Commission. Obedience came before anointing. Actually, it's probably only in the last couple of years that I could actually say that I am an evangelist. But I wasn't always. My experience is obedience came quite a few years before the anointing of an evangelist.

I am actually amazed in these days the open Heaven I have with the young people of Hobart. This is the Lord's doing and His Spirit has anointed me to do what I do.

Be willing to open your mouth and obey the Great Commission even if you don't feel that it's really your calling. You just never know what God can do with your willingness to be available.

## Training Others

After sharing the Gospel with thousands of people the next step for me was to start training others. That is how we will see multiplication. I have done this individually out on the streets and also for the last 2 years since writing my Fearless Evangelism seminar. I have shared the basics of evangelism with groups of people. In the seminar we also have time set aside for everyone to have a go at sharing the Gospel with a team mate. Hands on training in the seminar is a good way to put into practice what has been learnt.

On-the-street training has been a mixed bag for us. It works well when someone comes with a teachable spirit to observe and learn. My friend Bronte was a willing student and it went exceptionally well. God graciously led us to a back-slidden Christian first who was happy for Bronte to practise on her. We then passed a couple of guys in a laneway and again Bronte shared with them. It was such a blessing to me to train Bronte and see her step out and share the Gospel.

Unfortunately not everyone is like Bronte. We have had people who have come to us for training who just totally ignored everything we said. They often spent valuable time talking about themselves, or talking to teenagers like they're 2-year- olds, or even being judgmental and verbally aggressive, perhaps from nervousness. We often take people on the streets for training after they've participated in the Fearless Evangelism seminar and we have found so far that that has cut out the negative experiences. The first time I take someone out I ask them not to talk at all but just observe, although I may invite them to pray for the person or share some testimony.

The second time out I may get them doing the approach to initiate a conversation or maybe have a go at sharing the Gospel if they are ready for that. Then after a few times, I'll just do the observing and they do everything.

## Discipleship = Multiplication

If you disciple one person every 3 years and that person disciples someone new every 3 years then in 30 years that will be 1024 disciples. If you're discipling 3 people every 3 years and they do the same in 30 years that'll be 1,048,576 disciples. And if you're like Jesus and you disciple 12 every 3 years and they do the same then in 30 years that'll be more than double the population of the world now! Multiplication will happen when we train others and they do what we do. This book is a part of that vision. If I taught one person to share the Gospel and then they never taught anyone and I then trained another and again they didn't train anyone then we are only going to see some addition into the kingdom of God. But if I train someone and then they go train someone and I keep training others and they all go and train others then we will see real multiplication.

*"And the things that you have heard from me among many witnesses, commit these to faithful men who will be able to teach others also."* 2 Timothy 2:2

## Story of Matilda

Matilda comes to our church. She attended four Fearless Evangelism seminars before getting the courage to share the Gospel with someone she was seated next to on the bus on the way home from her fourth training seminar. She then decided to go to an old people's home and sit with some of the old people and share about Jesus. The first day she went she was there an hour having shared the Gospel with four old ladies.

Unfortunately the third lady she shared with got offended by the Gospel message and reported Matilda to the manager.

Matilda was asked to leave and never come back. Not to be put off, Matilda decided to continue being available to share the Gospel at the beach near where she lives for an hour every week. She's had mixed responses but she was determined and willing to have a go and be available for God.

## Love Hobart Highlights- 6th September 2016

On Tuesday there was a guy sitting by himself with his hoodie on leaning forward on his phone. I couldn't see who it was but I did sense I was supposed to talk to him. I went and sat down next to him. I'd never met him before but straight away he was engaging. This was one of the best talks about Jesus I've ever had. He was 21, from the mainland, and traveling with his cousin in a van around Australia. Having been in Tasmania for 5 months, they were leaving Hobart that afternoon. I spent 40 minutes with him and he was the most polite, gentle guy and so open to listen and talk. After I had prayed for him he thanked me so much for stopping to chat and he said that my talk with him had made his day. He was also looking forward to reading the Bible I gave him. Later I saw an 18 year old I knew, who's wanting to get on track with God. I talked with him and prayed and invited him to dinner and Bible study at our home that evening. He came. After talking with him I shared about Jesus with two shop assistants who had had some bad experiences with a Christian in the Mall. They were lovely and they were both really happy to take Bibles and tracts. Then I saw two 16 year olds, one who was crying. I didn't know them but gently asked what was wrong. I was able to share Jesus and pray and they too willingly took Bibles. As I was crossing the road, Mac was crossing in the opposite direction to me so I turned around and turned back with him as he wanted to talk. He is 15 years old and homeless. He introduced me to his friends, about six of them. Then I took him and three of his friends to a café for wedges and 'God-talk'. Later on I went to the park. It started raining so I asked the kids that were there if they would like to come for wedges and 'God-talk'. They said they didn't want to as they didn't want me spending my money on them. I explained to them they're not making me spend money on them but I'm happy to feed them. So they changed their minds. We had some good chats at the café and relationships are being built. One of the Mums of two of the girls I know text me to say that she is very encouraged to see her girls and the others speak so highly of me and my family.

Youth night was one of the best nights ever. We had a good turnout. One of the kids said there was such a good feel at Youth; a really good atmosphere. On Sunday a quarter of the people at church were contacts from street ministry. One 16 year old guy who came for the first time text me later to thank me. He said he enjoyed church and hanging out with our family as he could see we didn't swear or anything and he wants to change and hang out with us more. He then sent me a text about 10:45pm saying he'd had a nightmare so I text him a prayer he could say. Another kid put on Facebook he was stressed, so I encouraged him to talk to Jesus. He said he'd never done that but he would give it a go. One of the girls said to me yesterday that they all look forward to catching up with me in town and coming to Youth. Slowly but surely we are moving forward. May God's kingdom come to Hobart.

## Jesus was Patient in His Discipling

The disciples often did the wrong thing. They slept when they should have stayed awake, they got anxious when they should have just trusted and they argued about which of them was the greatest. This could have been quite frustrating for Jesus, yet He always showed them amazing patience. He never laughed at them or told them they were stupid, although He did tell His disciples when they were walking in unbelief. This was to encourage them to step up in faith. In His patience towards His disciples, Jesus showed self-control, gentleness and love which are all fruit of the Spirit.

God is so patient with us, often more than we deserve. Think of all the times God has been patient towards you: when you fail to spend time with Him, when you walk in unbelief and when you grumble. As the Lord is patient towards us, we need to be patient towards others. This can be especially true when discipling someone. A new Christian will not know what you know, they will not have the maturity that comes from a long standing relationship with the Lord. You will need to reflect Jesus to these young ones which will include patience. When they make mistakes, encourage them to get back up. When they fail at something, encourage them to try again. Be like Christ to them. Love them, encourage them, train them and lead by example.

## Outreach

We have also done a free sausage sizzle outreach in Franklin Square over a few Saturdays. This was really well received and we shared the Gospel with a lot of people, including a biker group that came through, who took up a donation for us on the spot. It's just so amazing when things like that happen.

## Sketches

One Youth night in June 2016, I took along my sketch pad. I thought I'd sit and do some artwork if it was a quiet night. I was sitting sketching a bird whilst next to Ray when I suddenly had the inspiration to ask if I could sketch him. He was quite happy at the thought of a pencil sketch so I took some photos and there began my series of the 'Faces of Love Hobart'. I started off taking 3 1/2 to 4 hours to do a sketch but the more I did the quicker I got. I'm now doing them in 1 1/2 to 2 hours on an A3 sheet of paper. I'm looking forward to having an art exhibition in June 2017 to showcase some of these pictures and more. Some of the sketches are on the cover design on the front of this book.

I've done maybe forty or so sketches now and it's been amazing the reaction to the sketches. I always give the kids their portrait sketch in a frame and they are just so appreciative. Often out on the streets now when I talk to young people that I don't know, someone will ask if I'm the lady who does the sketches.

## Story of Henry

One young guy that I met on the streets came to Youth one night. He was always a bit distant and didn't really want to talk, but he was only 15 years old. As he got to know us, he started opening up more. Sometimes he would bring a few of his friends to church. One Sunday after church we had pizzas in the park and Henry and his friends came in my car. Henry called my car 'the God car' with 'the God music'. On the way home that night Henry asked if I could speed. I don't speed, but I said I could take off a bit faster than usual. He pretended to get scared, so I locked the central locking. He then faked trying to escape out the window. There were a lot of laughs all around. It can be very helpful to have a sense of humour.

As I've shared many times in this book, I often take kids to a café for wedges and 'God talk'. I'll share Bible stories and it's just so amazing to share about Jonah and the big fish, or David and Goliath or Bible stories that they have never heard before. So I am doing a lot of discipling even if these young ones aren't saved yet. Sometimes God works in a different order to what we may naturally think should happen.

## Messages from some of my young friends

Over the years I've had some lovely messages of appreciation from some of the kids and some beautiful acts of kindness.

Following is a little sample. May they put a smile on your face as you read them.

## 12th August 2016

'Happy birthday Helen, thank you for helping me when I was in the rough spots last year, I appreciate it all. Your prayers must of really worked you deserve everything you wanted. I don't go to town anymore but I do hope to catch up with you soon, best wishes.' MS

My birthday was on a Friday night in 2016. When we started Youth there were a few kids that came in, but about 20 minutes later heaps of them rocked up. They wanted to honour me for my birthday and one of the girls I've known for quite some time walked in with a big bunch of flowers and a box of chocolates. What a blessing these kids are.

## 16th October 2016

'Thank you Helen, not just for today but everything you have done for me and the people of Hobart I know I will definitely see you again before I leave and I feel very blessed to have met you and your family!' TR

## 18th December 2016

'Thank you for everything you've done for me and everyone else this year you don't get enough credit for what you do you don't judge the scums like everyone else and we really appreciate that thank you so much again. Thank you again Helen you're a true legend.' CM

## 25th December 2016

'Merry Christmas Helen! Thank you for everything you've done for me over the last 7 months! Very appreciative to have had you help me and so blessed to have met such a kind soul both like yourself and your family! I'll see you at Youth after the holidays!' HR

## Bibles

There have been times where I've given out as many as 30 Bibles in a week and they're all to people I share the Gospel with first. Most people I give Bibles to have never owned one before. I've even had kids come and ask me for Bibles on a number of occasions. Often they may see their friends Bibles and they want one too.

The Gospel of the Bible is our standard, our anchor. We need to preach the same Gospel that's in the Bible. Any other Gospel is not the truth. After Jesus rose again and appeared to two of the disciples on the road to Emmaus, He shared the Scriptures and not His experience *(Luke 24:25-27)*. When the Holy Spirit came at Pentecost and those full of the Holy Spirit were mocked, Peter didn't try telling them about His experience, but about Jesus Christ, Him crucified and risen again *(Acts 2)*. Philip didn't share his experience in Samaria of all the healings, miracles and deliverances with the Ethiopian Eunuch, but he preached Jesus to Him *(Acts 8:35)*. We need to have a passion to share Jesus even more than our testimony. The only way into God's Kingdom is through Jesus. It is a work of the Holy Spirit. Sowing seeds can take time and we won't always see the fruit immediately. But we will see fruit eventually, if we don't give up.

*"The hard working farmer must be first to partake of the crops." 2 Timothy 2:6*

*"And let us not grow weary while doing good, for in due season we shall reap if we do not lose heart." Galatians 6:9*

*"Do not be deceived, God is not mocked; for whatever a man sows that he will also reap." Galatians 6: 7*

*"Those who sow in tears shall reap in joy. He who continually goes forth weeping, bearing seed for sowing, shall doubtless come again with rejoicing, bringing his sheaves with him." Psalm 126:5-6*

Use wisdom. Be sensitive to the Spirit and to your team members as to what they sense. Use team work. It's not about you doing all you want to do, but it is about God doing all He wants to do. Can you wait and pray even if that means you have to stand back and pray quietly while your team member gets to do all the interaction?

## Love Hobart Update- 31st October 2016

Last Monday night one of the kids came to prayer meeting and he stayed for the whole hour! On Tuesday I caught up with him and his friend for 'God-talk' in a café for 1 ½ hrs. They both told me their story and how they've come to be in shelters at the moment. There is always lots of rejection in these stories. My heart goes out to them. One kid shared how he came off his skateboard earlier that morning. He sat down, as he was in pain, and took his Bible that I gave him a couple of days earlier out his backpack. He opened it randomly and started reading in Acts about Peter healing people. He asked me if I knew about Peter. I said, "Yes." He then went on to say that as he kept reading about Peter the pain he had from his fall went away.

How faithful is God! Later I talked to a couple in the Mall from South Korea. They had moved to Hobart 3 days earlier for study. They were

Christians. I prayed for them to settle in well. I talked with a Youth who was from a Christian home. He said he was turned off Christianity by hypocrisy he saw in his home. Later I saw Mick who'd hurt his hand. I prayed for his hand there and then. He was with three others so we all went to a coffee shop for wedges and 'God-talk'. Two of the girls had a falling out with someone else and wanted to talk about that. After they'd finished I talked to them about forgiveness and not holding a grudge and shared how God forgives us. We then had four guys to our home for dinner: two from the shelter who have been once before. I had a 'heavy' talk with one on spiritual warfare. On Friday, Shalom and I talked to two girls from Friends school. They were very inquisitive. They both took tracts. After sharing the Gospel with a few others we went to the park where there were lots of chats. Later in the Mall, I met a girl I knew who was feeling very low so I spent ½ hour or more doing some prayer ministry for inner healing with her. She used to walk with Jesus and she is making steps back to Him. We arrived at Youth early and so did a few of the kids. A 16 year old we know well who hadn't been to Youth for ages came in with his girlfriend. Unbeknown to us there had been a big ding dong between him and one of the other kids who came a bit later. This meant half the young people were seated outside the building and wouldn't come in as there had been a big division between them. After some talk on forgiveness and being an intermediary between the two groups, inside and out, the kids outside all came in. They were all civil towards each other, thankfully! Some did choose to leave earlier than normal though, but at least they came. What a night! After Youth I took three of the African guys to Woollies as one needed to do his food shopping and wanted help. (Three weeks earlier he'd been swearing at me for bringing some correction. Now he's calling me Mum again!) I got home at 10:30pm! Then on Saturday I ran two work shops on evangelism at the Tasmanian Anglican conference on making disciples. Both my sessions were booked out which was great and Shalom spoke in both sessions too. Sunday I preached on growing in peace and there were four kids from street ministry there including one who'd never been to church before. Life is full on and it sometimes feels like a crazy journey but Jesus is with us in this ministry.

## Love Hobart Update- 3rd April 2017

On Tuesday Brook text me to catch up. I shared some of my sermon from Sunday with her and then two others joined us. I got Brook and Graham to go through the EvangeCube for Tim who hadn't heard the Gospel before and of course I prayed for them all. As I left the café I opened the door for two ladies with a baby in a pram and I was able to share with them. They both took Bibles and tracts, just like that! I later shared the Gospel with a 30 year old Muslim from Iraq who's been in Hobart three weeks. He wanted me to walk him to where church meets as he was interested to come. I later went to the park with pizzas and shared the Gospel using the EvangeCube with a new kid. I also prayed for healing for a couple of kids who were in pain: one in their ankle and one in their back. Two guys came back for dinner and Bible study. James also recommitted his life to the Lord on Saturday night and after church he was very keen to talk and have some deliverance ministry. There was also a young Mum who really wanted prayer after church too. As we prayed the tears came. She's at the beginning of her journey with Jesus. And then there was Friday! Shalom came out with me on the streets again. Every person we talked to was open and we gave out quite a few more Bibles. As I shared with a guy in motorbike gear (with a suit on underneath as he'd just been for a job interview), an 18 year old girl came and sat in the seat behind us. Shalom saw she was crying, so when we got up to leave Rick, having given him a Bible and a tract, Shalom whispered to me about the girl. She was on the phone so we waited until she'd finished then went and asked her if she was Ok. Amy was upset because she'd been bullied and she was frightened those people would find her. She has been suicidal and in and out of hospital. I went and bought her Subway while Shalom waited with her. With her permission, I shared the cube while she ate and then we walked with her to her bus and saw her safely on the bus. She was very grateful.

## Walking in the Kingdom

We can use our feet to walk where Jesus sends us. We can use our hands to show the Kingdom by laying hands on the sick, hugging and helping. We can use our mouth to share the Gospel and to declare the awesome wonders of our God, His love, His grace, His mercy, and His truth. Walk in confidence that God goes before you, while remembering that you have the Holy Spirit within you to empower you as you preach the Word, lay hands on the sick and testify of the things of the kingdom of God.

As a Christian, it's not so much about how we start our journey with Jesus but how we finish. Are you running your race well for Jesus? Are you sharing the Gospel? Are you moving forward? Or are you slowly giving up? Being a Christian is not easy. Opposition will come. Discouragement will come.

Temptations will come. Distractions will come. Persecution will come. But through it all, we have the Lord Jesus Christ to strengthen us and help us if we will continue on.

*"I can do all things through Christ who strengthens me."* *Philippians 4:13*

*"But sanctify the Lord God in your hearts, and always be ready to give a defence to everyone who asks you a reason for the hope that is in you, with meekness and fear."*

*1 Peter 3:15*

*"Give me one hundred preachers who fear nothing but sin, and desire nothing but God, and I care not a straw whether they be clergymen or laymen; such alone will shake the gates of Hell and set up the kingdom of Heaven on earth."*

*John Wesley*

# Chapter 9

# Frequently Asked Questions and Answers

One reason that Christians are often too scared to try and share the Gospel is the fear of not having all the answers. You don't need to have all the answers! You just need humility to be able to say I don't know the answer to that question but I can try and find out for you.

## Story

One Sunday afternoon I arrived at church ready to set up. I wasn't feeling too good that day. Even before I got out of my car, I text a couple of my friends to pray for me. As I walked through the lane there were three groups of kids there. As I walked into church my family encouraged me to go talk to some of them. I really felt unwell but I knew I should go and see who I could talk to. When I went back outside the two smaller groups had gone and there was just one group of seven university students there. I introduced myself and so began a very intense one hour conversation. I shared the Gospel but was also bombarded with loads of questions, specifically to do with ethics. I couldn't answer all the questions although I answered quite a few. I acknowledged I didn't know all the answers, but I could try and find out. They were very passionate about what they believed and two of them in particular were very forthright. But interestingly at the end of our conversation five of them took Bibles and the other two already owned Bibles. They also let me pray a blessing over them. Then the guy that had been the most antagonistic thanked me for talking and said that I shouldn't be put off by his manner as he actually thought what I do on the streets was great and he encouraged me to keep doing it!

Another time I received an email from someone I'd met on the streets a few days earlier. The email was full of a wide variety of questions. This was somewhat easier to respond to as I could take my time in answering the questions and search out the answers. We don't need to know everything, we just need to be humble.

Following are some answers to commonly asked questions about God, the Bible and Jesus.

## Why Does God Allow Bad Things To Happen?

Death is not a natural thing but a spiritual consequence for sin (*Romans 6:23*). The wages of sin is death. There was no death before sin entered the world. When sin entered the world all of creation became cursed, even the ground. The suffering we see now is a warning of the judgement that has begun, but is also to come. Sin brings death and suffering.

But there is hope (*Revelation 21:4*). Death will be no more. Things will be restored better at the end of the age than they were originally. Although the curse is great, the answer is greater. The answer is Jesus. He became a curse for us so that all who call on His name will be saved. None of us deserve what Jesus did for us. He is love, and He showed His love.

# I'm Not a Bad Person, and God's a Forgiving God Isn't He?

There is none good, no not one. Sometimes we compare ourselves with others and feel that we are quite good, at least, better than most others. But the standard that applies is God's standard of righteousness which also involves inner purity.

Have you obeyed the greatest commandment, "to love the Lord your God with all your heart, mind, soul and strength?"

We have all sinned against God which means we have all fallen short of His perfection. Do you know what God did for us so we can have eternal life with Him? He sent His Son Jesus to die on the cross as a substitute for us so that all who call on His name will be saved.

## Does God Hate Homosexuals?

God does NOT hate homosexuals, or those practising any sin, or people of other religions for that matter, and neither do we. Amazingly, God loves sinners and offers terms of peace.

*"For God so loved the world, that He gave his only begotten son, that whoever believes in Him should not perish, but have everlasting life. For God did not send His Son into the world to condemn the world, but that the world through Him might be saved." John 3: 16-17*

It is really a question of truth. Are we free to do whatever we want, or is there a higher standard of right and wrong (outside of man) that applies to us? If there is no higher standard, then there is no basis at all for right and wrong, but if we are created by a creator God, then He has the right to lay down the terms of how we are to live. He has said homosexuality is a sin, but so is sexual immorality and adultery. God is just, but He is also very loving. All who reject Jesus as Lord and Saviour will spend an eternity separated from God in Hell. That is justice for sin if there is no repentance. But all who receive Jesus Christ as Lord and Saviour will spend eternity with our God in Heaven. That is because of God's amazing grace, love and mercy.

## Story of My Friend Chris

The first time I met Chris was at the Rock café. He came in with a friend and after they had been at a table for a while I went and asked them if I could join them. They both nodded. It wasn't until Chris spoke that I realised he was actually a male dressed as a girl. Anyway I continued my conversation with him and his friend, sharing the Gospel with them both. Later that evening Chris came back to the café with some other friends.

As the weeks went on, Chris would come to the Rock most Fridays. He was homeless at the time and later he told us, the Rock was a refuge for him where he could come and get warm, be fed, encouraged and not judged.

One Friday, Chris brought in a new friend with him to the café. It was a particularly busy time at the café and although he wanted me to talk with him and his friend they were happy to wait while I finished talking to others. Chris picked up an EvangeCube from the coffee table and put it on their table, ready for me to share with him and his friend. That was very encouraging to see.

When I came to sit with Chris and his friend they were eagerly waiting for me to go through the cube. As I opened the cube to the second picture of Jesus on the cross Chris asked me a question, "Can homosexuals go to Heaven?" My reply was this: "nobody with sin can go to Heaven." No matter what sin we have done, all sin stops us going to Heaven. Chris understood that.

As we came to know Chris more, I thought I should invite him to church. Sure enough, he showed up one week. He had bright blue hair, lots of jewels, all dressed up for church. We asked him to sit with us in the front and he did. He stayed and had dinner after, and he commended me on my preaching and then David dropped him home. He is such a precious young guy who we love dearly.

When the café closed, I text Chris to come by for our last day, but he didn't come. A couple of weeks later though I received this text message from him.

"Hello Helen, its Chris. Sorry I wasn't able to make it to see you all off or get back to you sooner. I just wanted to write to you to thank you, your family, and everyone at The Rock for everything you have done for me. You guys really were a lifesaver. Coming in after a night on the streets in the cold to a hot coffee, much needed food and friendly faces really was a blessing for myself and Lucy, and many others. Words can't even express how much that meant to us. Thank you again for your ongoing support and everything you have done for me.

You guys did a wonderful service to the people of Hobart. Much love, and endless support for all your future endeavours. Sincerely, Chris."

We then lost touch with Chris for about a year. We later found out his phone had been smashed, he'd lost all the contact details and so couldn't contact us. But one day as I was walking through town I saw a young guy in a leather jacket, very much dressed as a male but I knew it was Chris. I called out to him and he turned around, and yes, it was him. We had a hug and chat. I asked him if he had time for a coffee, and he did, so off we went to a coffee shop for an hour or so to catch up on all the happenings of the last year. Chris told me of a run in he'd had with a Christian preacher on the streets which was quite sad. Then Chris told me how much he appreciated us loving him where he was at. He said our care of him was like a fly being drawn to honey rather than being repelled by vinegar.

A couple of weeks later Chris came to church again. As we were singing the final song after the sermon, Chris came up and whispered to me, could he say a few words. Well that took me off guard. In that split second I had voices of other pastors going through my head warning me to be careful who I gave the microphone to. All I could think to say to Chris was, "Is it good?" He looked at me kindly and said, "Yes Helen." So when the song finished I stood up and told everyone Chris wanted to say something and that although I didn't know what it was I was going to let him speak.

This is what he said.

"I'd just like to take a moment to say a special thank you to Helen and her family for the work they have done and continue to do with the people of Hobart, and especially myself. I have known Helen and her family for about 3 years now, and where others have passed judgement, they have shown me nothing but love and acceptance. The work Helen has been doing with the troubled youth of the city resonates particularly powerfully with me, as when I met them I was experiencing homelessness myself as well as struggling with drug and alcohol problems. During this time, to be able to come in from the streets on a cold winters night to a hot drink and something to fill my stomach was truly a blessing, one I will always be grateful for. But what truly touched me was the way they welcomed me in with open arms, to a listening ear and heartfelt words from people who truly cared when it felt as though nobody else did. They saw me, not for my circumstances, or my outward appearances, nor for my sins or lack of faith, but for my heart, which through them I came to see was good. And for all that I am thankful in ways that words fail to describe. And while unfortunately I do not yet walk with God, I do however walk wholeheartedly with all of you which just goes to show you can catch more flies with honey than you do with vinegar. When Helen stands before us delivering her sermons you can tell she truly loves and believes in what she is doing. She glows with the fire of a woman who despite the adversities she faces is truly real in what she does."

Chris has started praying too, and not just for himself but for others. He's even been preaching and sharing about church and Jesus on Facebook. His friends' responses are, "what's wrong with you man?" He is a very precious young man, and my hope is that one day he will come to know Jesus. He's working full time now and moved out of town so even though we don't catch up that often, it's always lovely when we do.

## How Can You Know That You Have The Truth?

If there is a God as the Bible says, then He is able to reveal Himself to whomever He pleases. Actually, the only way that any of us will be able to arrive at truth is if one who knows truth reveals it to us. God has revealed Himself and His truth to us in a variety of ways: through His Word, the Bible, through prophecy, history, miracles, eye-witness accounts and an inner witness within our hearts which we call our conscience.

Conscience literally means, 'with knowledge'. The greatest revelation of truth was the incarnation of Jesus. That is, God became flesh and dwelt amongst us. This was not done in secret, but in real historical documented events that can be scrutinised by anyone who seriously seeks the truth.

## Who Made God?

In the very first verse of the Bible we read,

*"In the beginning God..." Genesis 1:1*

God has always been. He is eternal. To understand this fully is beyond our comprehension as we only know and understand time. God does not exist inside time, so there is no cause and effect. He is from everlasting to everlasting *(Psalm 90:2)*. So no-one made God. Perhaps this offends because it is not understandable, or it boggles your brain. The reality is that our world is not understandable. Who made matter? The answer is it came from energy. Who made energy then? The reality of our existence in all its complexity and wonder is not explainable, not even by science. This is why there must be an unexplainable source which the Bible reveals to us as God. (Thanks to my hubby David for helping write this answer.)

*"By faith we understand that the worlds were framed by the Word of God, so that the things which are seen were not made of things that were visible." Hebrews 11:3*

## Isn't Faith The Opposite of Science?

The essence of science is the scientific method which involves a hypothesis (theory), which is tested by experiments to either confirm or disprove its accuracy in describing reality. Science does not prove anything, it only confirms by experiment. Some theories are so well confirmed, we call them laws, but even some of our 'laws' are known to breakdown under certain conditions.

So to be scientific, let's formulate a hypothesis that there is a God that the Bible speaks of. Does the experimental data confirm or disprove God's existence? There is real experimental data within you: your own personhood. There are very few people who maintain that they are mere machines. Most of us know that we are a person, not an object. Our person-ness confirms the idea that there is a personal God who created us. You will find that there is a lot of experimental evidence that actually confirms the idea that the God of the Bible is reasonable. Take for instance the concepts of the 2nd Law of Thermodynamics which is the scientific way of describing that random chance does not produce the bewildering complexity of a living cell. (Thanks again to David for helping with this answer.)

*What About Other Religions, Are They All Wrong? Other religions may have elements of truth, but one point of difference will always be their treatment of who Jesus is.*

Without Jesus, the perfect Son of God, there is no remedy for the problem of sin. There is no other sacrifice acceptable to God's justice that can substitute or take away our sin except the perfect sacrifice: Jesus Himself, who died on the cross and was raised again the third day. Without this sacrifice, there is no mechanism for your sins to be forgiven and justice maintained at the same time. Without forgiveness of sins, we will face pure justice.

## Is The Devil Real?

Yes, the devil is as real as you and me. The devil was the worshipping angel who was cast out of Heaven by God because he got pride in his heart. He took a third of the angels with him. He now roams the earth and is described as the prince of the air, but his time is short. When Jesus died on the cross and was resurrected on the third day, He defeated the devil. Until the second coming of Jesus, Satan, the devil, is still roaming the earth seeking whom he may devour. He doesn't want anyone to go to Heaven as he knows he can't go there. He knows his eternal destiny is the lake of fire but until he is cast into the lake of fire he is intent on destroying mankind. But we have an advocate, Jesus, who intercedes for us day and night. There is a very real battle going on between God and His angels and Satan and his demons for the souls of mankind.

## What about Heaven and Hell are They Real?

Yes, both Heaven and Hell are real. They are outside of time. There are many examples of people who have experienced both Heaven and Hell but we also know from the Bible the reality of these two places. When someone dies, their spirit either goes to Heaven or to Hell. Heaven is for all those who repent and accept Jesus as their Lord and Saviour. Hell is for all who reject Jesus. At the end of time there will be the final judgement and all who are the Lord's will spend eternity with Him in the new Heaven and the new earth and all those who rejected Jesus will be thrown into the lake of fire. Even Hell itself will be thrown into the lake of fire.

*"And I saw the dead, small and great, standing before God, and books were opened. And another book was opened, which is the Book of Life. And the dead were judged according to their works, by the things that were written in the books. The sea gave up the dead who were in it, and Death and Hades delivered up the dead who were in them. And they were judged each one according to his works. Then Death and Hades were thrown into the lake of fire. This is the second death. And anyone not found written in the Book of Life was cast into the lake of fire." Revelation 20: 12–15*

## Have You Ever Done An Exorcism?

I have been asked this question so many times and it's the one question that really gets everyone's attention! I explain that exorcism is a catholic term and I do deliverance ministry.

Although Hollywood has overplayed what happens in an exorcism, it does open up the way for me to explain about deliverance ministry. When I do a deliverance it's always with the person's permission. I lead them through a prayer of repentance of any sin they have done to open up the door for an evil spirit to oppress them. Then in the Name of Jesus I bind the evil spirit and tell it to leave. I've even done this in coffee shops as it can, at times, be done quietly and without fuss.

## What is Deliverance?

It is freedom from demonic bondage, that is, to rescue from captivity. Deliverance then is to rescue from danger and bring victory. Deliverance is achieved by casting out evil spirits by authority and power in Jesus' Name. Jesus came to destroy the works of the devil *(1 John 3:8)*.

Examples of Jesus' deliverance ministry are found all through the Gospels. In *Mark 9:14-29* and *Matthew 17:14-21* we read of a scene of spiritual conflict and unbelief. This epileptic boy's symptoms were demonic and came with a deaf and dumb spirit. In Bible times the people recognised demons by their symptoms. It's not so likely today as we live in 'civilised' times. But demons can, and still do, dwell in people today. Often demons can be discerned by the behaviour of the person.

To be successful in deliverance ministry there must be trust in the Lord, who has all authority over the demons and who has given us that same authority. In the Great Commission in *Mark 16:15-20*, believers are commissioned to do the same as Jesus, yet very few believers cast out demons. Jesus destroyed the works of the devil and He has given us the power and authority to do the same *(John 14:12)*. When we command demons to leave they have to bow to the higher authority, and we have that authority in the Name of Jesus.

So there's a few of the most asked questions with answers to help you on your way to being brave, bold, prepared and equipped in sharing the Gospel and answering some of the questions that are likely to come up. But again, if you don't know the answer don't be afraid to say; just keep a humble heart.

*"But you shall receive power when the Holy Spirit has come upon you; and you shall be witnesses to Me in Jerusalem, and in all Judea, and Samaria, and to the end of the earth."*

*Acts 1:8*

*"I cannot tell you what joy it gave me to bring the first soul to the Lord Jesus Christ. I have tasted almost all the pleasures that this world can give... but those pleasures were as nothing compared to the joy that the saving of that ONE SOUL gave me."*

*C. T. Studd*

# Chapter 10

# Conclusion

Learning to share the Gospel is often a process. I didn't learn everything overnight. It's been a journey, some of which I've shared in this book. Have a teachable spirit and be willing to be trained again and again until you know the Gospel well. That is, until you can't help but speak of Jesus and the cross. Be willing to obey the Great Commission. Learn how to share the Gospel then practise. Practise on your kids, your grandkids, your pets, anyone who will let you. And then expect God to use you.

It is the 'hearing' of the Gospel that will bring people into God's Kingdom. I trust this book has inspired you and encouraged you to carry out the mission of the Kingdom of God to GO into all the world and preach the Gospel.

*"How then shall they call on Him in whom they have not believed? And how shall they believe in Him of whom they have not heard? And how shall they hear without a preacher?" Romans 10:14*

*What is the Gospel? (In case it hasn't sunk in yet.) Simply put: "…that Christ died for our sins according to the Scriptures' and that He was buried, and that He rose again the third day according to the Scriptures." 1 Corinthians 15:3-4*

Where can you start sharing the Gospel? Even if you're scared and you fumble your way through your first few times of sharing the Gospel, keep a look out for opportunities. God will help you. For example, you could be on a walk at the beach and there's a bench chair that you sit down to have a rest on. Not long after, someone comes and sits next to you. That could very well be a God opportunity to share the Gospel. I've had that exact thing happen to me.

Are you passionate about Jesus, the cross and all that He has done for you? In other words, would people want what you've got? If you're not passionate, get passionate. Get intimate with the Lord. Ignite the passion in your heart through intimate relationship in Jesus. You'll know there's a change when you just want to talk about Him and how great He is and what He's done for you. Draw near to the Lord. Read His Word. Praise Him, adore Him, give thanks to Him, love Him, and spend time with Him. I want people to want what I have: a living, personal, intimate relationship with the Living God. Don't you?

*"Preach the Word! Be ready in season and out of season. Convince, rebuke, exhort, with all long suffering and teaching." 2 Timothy 4:2*

This is a planting season. If you don't plant during the planting season you won't reap a harvest. But are you also willing to plant and sow seeds into people that you may never reap a harvest from personally? That could be tourists and backpackers, people you meet on the bus, a taxi driver, someone at the beach. It requires maturity to do that. Just be willing to be part of God's team and do your part in His kingdom no matter the earthly rewards. For there will be an eternal reward for your willing obedience and faithfulness to GO!

I wonder how long we have until we're banned from sharing the Gospel publicly, and even privately. Are we making the most of the freedoms we have now, while we can? We have this window of opportunity to still preach the Gospel without fear of fines, imprisonment or anything else at the moment, but it may not always be like that.

Renew your mind by seeing people through the Father's eyes of love. They are lost and heading to Hell. God doesn't want to see them go to

Hell and neither should we. The Holy Spirit will help you to proclaim BOLDLY the Gospel, if you are willing.

Be available! I don't just share the Gospel on my days out on the streets. I'm always on the lookout for anyone I can talk to about Jesus, even on phone calls. Be available even when you're busy. Be available when you're tired. Be available even when you don't feel like sharing the Gospel. And then watch God move through you. What a privilege to be able to preach the Gospel.

Be ready! Carry tracts and Bibles with you in your bag or pocket, and in your car. Have an expectancy that God will use you even if you think you've muffed up or you don't know enough yet, don't give up and don't hold back. Have a go. God may just use you if you're available.

Be clothed in humility for *"God resists the proud but gives grace to the humble." (1 Peter 5:5).* You will have trouble getting anyone to listen to you if you're puffed up with pride and arrogance. Walk in the fruit of the Spirit and let your manner speak as much as your message.

*"Let all that you do be done with love."* 1 Corinthians 16:14

I have met some of the most amazing people while doing street ministry, especially the youth of Hobart. Through my willingness and obedience to go onto the streets of Hobart to share the Gospel, I have been blessed. I love these young people so very much. There is so much God-potential in each one of them. They are all precious, as I often tell them and my heart's desire is that one day each of them will come to a saving knowledge of Jesus Christ as Lord and Saviour; that none would be lost. Until then, I continue to feed them, physically and spiritually, I love them, share the Gospel with them and pray for them daily. I trust that in doing this, I am reflecting Jesus to them and preparing the way for a mighty move of God's Spirit in this city and beyond.

If you have been touched by any of the real life stories in this book please pray for those individuals. Names have been changed for privacy, but the Lord knows them by name. The power of prayer is real so if you will pray along with us for these precious young people may we see the harvest come in due season.

## Final Word

Be available.
Be willing.
Be teachable.
Be obedient.
Be sensitive to the Holy Spirit.
Then be ready to go and give God the glory for what He does in and through you!
Let's GO!

## To be continued …

# Bibliography

Bartleman, Frank *'Azusa Street – An Eyewitness Account to the Birth of the Pentecostal Revival'* 1982, Whitaker House.

Chant, Ken *'Equipped to Serve'*, 1995; Vision College; registrar@visioncolleges.net

Comfort, Ray 'Way of the Master', *www.livingwaters.com*

'EvangeCube' available from *www.e3resources.org*

Finny, Charles, cited by Duncan Campbell *'The Price and Power of Revival.'*

Murray, Andrew *'The Ministry of Intercessory Prayer'*, 1981, Bethany House.

Piper, John *'Don't waste your life'*, 2003, Crossway Books.

Platt, David *'Radical: Taking back your faith from the American dream'* 2010.

Spurgeon, Charles Haddon *'She was not Hid'*, Sermon at Metropolitan Tabernacle, 1888.

Stott, John *'Lausanne Covenant'*, Paragraph 4, 1974.

Studd, C. T. *'C. T. Studd Cricketer & Pioneer'*, by Norman Grubb, 1933

Wesley, John from a letter to Alexander Mather, 1777

www.ingramcontent.com/pod-product-compliance
Lightning Source LLC
LaVergne TN
LVHW051404080426
835508LV00022B/2960